CHRISTOPHER MALONEY

WILDCARD

A Wild Wolf Publication

Published by Wild Wolf Publishing in 2018

Copyright © 2018 Christopher Maloney & Tony Horne

First print

All opinions are the personal opinions of the author.

ISBN: 978-1-907954-70-2
Also available as an e-book

www.wildwolfpublishing.com

Acknowledgements

I dedicate this book to my beautiful mother, Pat, who has been there through everything – my Mum and my best friend. Dad, too – despite the honest tensions I portray in the following pages! My sister, Tricia – my rock. I love you to bits. And Gary – my partner, rather than Gary Barlow – what a *journey*. My Nan, obviously, I owe you the earth, you little star.

My friends: I love you always. Constant and consistent all the time.

Special thanks go to Stuart and Kim Rawlinson, who believed in me from the start, and of course you for supporting me and anyone who ever voted for me. To Miss Groves, my drama teacher, I am so grateful that you nurtured me. To the people of Liverpool, thank you. You are right. I never did walk alone.

From my first audition until today, you remain my level playing field. I love my city and its salt of the earth people.

To my trolls who thought you could hide behind fake usernames and still continue to pursue my poorly Nan in her late 80s, just have a think about what you have done. Learn from the story within these pages and understand that I now know that it is reflection on you not me!

To the press too, I do make some observations about a small minority of you in this book who took the easy line and re-distributed some pretty poor narrative. Some of this made me very ill.

But, I stress that 99% of you have been a pleasure to deal with and I am grateful that we have a decent working relationship that I also highlight and I look forward to continuing that. Thank you for my enormous column issues!

To all the TV shows who continue to support me, I am also delighted to be an honorary Loose Woman. Love you guys!

Special mentions go to the team at Beresford Management, my academy students and of course, Aesthetics Practitioner, Neil from Skin Appeal Clinic, who keeps me glowing whenever I am in Liverpool! I will add to that my fabulous surgeons (including Bridgette) at Europe Surgery and Marwan Saifi from Saifi Hair Transplant Centre in Poland.

To my former colleagues from LMH, I miss you dearly and thank you for being you.

My friends Denise and Stuart Fergus – I am a proud patron of your wonderful charity 'James Bulger Memorial Trust'. Thank you for *your* friendship.

To my writing team, thanks to my brilliant editor, Tony Horne, who has turned this book around in no time at all. If you google him, you will see he is a class act with around 20 books to his credit. If you have a story, I recommend you email him at books@tonyhornebooks.com. I bet he does not edit that bit out. Ah, I see he has not.

In turn he owes gratitude to his researcher, John Iley and his proof reader, Matt Rance (@proofprofessor), who do the magic for us.

Thanks also to Rod Glenn and the team at Wild Wolf Publishing who said yes to this book in an instant.

My final word is to you, the reader. I am truly humbled that you still follow my story. I am duty bound to ask you to post a review on Amazon and ask you to use the hashtag Wildcard, but I understand that it is like Big Brother asking you to see if my words have the X Factor or not!

I hope you enjoy this. And thank you for reading.

Much Love,

Christopher Maloney
12 November 2018.

I see a shooting star for the first time in my life. I am at Boughton House in the Northamptonshire countryside and it is late in the evening in the summer of 2012. I tell myself it is a sign. They will definitely put me through.

They don't.

Gary Barlow and Cheryl Cole tell me the next day that I have not made it into the live shows of this year's *X Factor*. On television, I am devastated. The words that come out of my mouth do not ring true.

In fact, I am actually hugely relieved, satisfied that I have got this far. I have done my best and my best is not quite good enough on this occasion. I do not feel empty, just hollow because of all the strain of the process. I can finally go home.

Then, a twist.

Gary tells me that, after all this, he wants me to go through as his wildcard entry where the public get to pick one final act from each of the judges' rejects. I am back in the game.

All I ever really wanted to do was stand on the X on that world-famous stage and two weeks later on a Saturday night, I am there singing to save myself when the competition hasn't really begun at all.

Dermot O'Leary introduces me on stage along with all the other hopefuls. A quick outfit change and deliver *Hero* by Mariah Carey. As they say often on this show, I *nail it*.

I begin to re-think. I *do* want this after all and I want it more than ever now. Something has changed. I recognise a potentially more level playing field in the live shows.

I am made to wait 24 hours until the Sunday show to find out my fate.

The next day, I line up backstage with the other wildcards. Then Dermot announces my name. I am through after all. My knees turn to jelly and my body hits the deck. The mental exhaustion and anxiety rise to the fore – this is an old problem of mine and now the public can see it too for the first time.

It is a defining moment. And I am ecstatic. I realise instantly that once the decision is put in the public's hands, they have voted me overwhelmingly *in*. I get that instantly. The public are honest and had faith.

I am aware too that no wildcard has ever won the show, nor are they likely to. In my mind, that could make a mockery of the judging process. Surely, you can't have a show like this where somebody who was initially rejected goes on to win.

But I was in. I had made it – and take a massive vote of confidence from the endorsement of the viewers, whilst casting a nervous look over my shoulder at the enormous process ahead of me.

I am stunned that Bette Midler herself had tweeted me, even taking the time to find my username and tag me in:

'Just saw the incredible triumph of @ChrisMaloney77 on @TheXFactor UK singing *The Rose* ... congratulations! Keep it up!!'

Wow. I was blown away – Bette Midler commenting on her own track about the song that means the most to me. Yet, somehow you don't always hear the praise.

They originally didn't want me on the show. Gary Barlow seemed to make a case for me. I gained over 63% of that first vote – but, in the back of my mind, I felt that throughout my entire life I had never been wanted, and had always been excluded right from an early age. So, my confidence was low. But at least, I was in. I was now the *wildcard.*

Chapter One

I was born in Scottie Road, Liverpool in 1977. I already had a sister Tricia who was one year older. My Mum, Pat, was a cleaner. Chris, my father, worked in security on a building site. It was a rough, tough area and home was a small maisonette on a council estate. We had nothing.

My parents worked all hours to make sure we had *something* at birthdays and Christmas time. Holidays were rare and no further than Blackpool. Oddly, my father would never come. Dad was a man's man and Tricia was his little girl. I was very close, almost clingy to Mum.

I remember starting out at Infants School and just balling my eyes out on the way. Mum reassured me it would be fine, but the fact that I never really took to education began before I had even got there on that first day. And from that point on, I was bullied – right the way from the age of five until some time after I left twelve years later.

I don't know how it started and I didn't really understand it until much later *but* I was always playing with the girls and joining in dancing. I didn't really have any friends and certainly none amongst the boys. Some of my classmates clearly took this home and told their parents and then those kids brought it back in and started calling me the little queer – words, really that at that age, could have only come from an external influence, like an older generation for whom it was very much the language of the day.

There was a lot of casual racism too. I hated every minute of school. Once it started, it then followed me into the Juniors and onto Secondary School. Nobody questioned it and I couldn't do anything about it. If I told the teachers, they accused me of being disruptive. There was no way I could mention anything to Dad. There was some distance between us – the generational gap in the 1980s was still huge. His upbringing and the culture in society was that people were able to be racist and homophobic and there was no proper recourse for addressing it. You just got on with it and had to endure. As I write this in 2018, obviously the world has changed and I recently ran into one of my bullies in Liverpool who was man enough to apologise. I told him it was fine, but then when I thought about it, it really wasn't at all. I now understand that abuse to the extent that I received without any way of addressing it can make the abused person accepting of it. You know no different and ultimately become immune. That is why I told him it was fine years later. It wasn't fine at all.

Mum knew I was different, though we never spoke about it. Once, she caught me playing with my sister's *Barbie* dolls. I was always watching the glamorous over the top, and perhaps slightly camp American shows like *Dynasty* and *The Colbys*. Sometimes, I would withdraw to my bedroom and make up little plays or re-enact *Coronation Street* or sit at the desk with a big sheet across the wall pinned to the artex ceiling as though I was in some sort of studio. Here, I would pretend to be a radio presenter. And I would often stay inside for days.

Many of my actions were probably meeting the stereotype of 'gay'. I didn't understand what it meant. I just was aware that I felt different inside. It seemed totally natural to dance with the girls at school and play with dolls at home. I was only a kid after all.

As a result, I was routinely beaten. To avoid this, and to make people like me, I tried to make the bullies laugh, but it rarely worked. The only time there was any kind of let-off was in drama classes when *they* needed to look good and begged me to be in their group because they knew it was my forte. I would duly accept as the only respite from their attacks.

My only decent memory of school is therefore drama. The teacher, Mrs Groves, took a shine to me too, which I lived for. I would write plays and music and she would always encourage me and allow me to perform them for the school. When it came to the productions, I wanted to be involved in every way I could, from helping backstage, to costume design. I wrote the entire script the year we did *Aladdin*.

This really was the beginning and end of my education. Two themes manifested themselves at a very early age. The performing arts were where my heart lay, and bullying was going to be a permanent problem.

I kept much of the drama from my Dad. I knew it was not for him and he would not approve. I would tell Mum that I wanted to go into town to rehearse and she would discreetly iron a couple of shirts for me, leave me £7 to cover costs and make sure I never spoke of it. Once, at the age of twelve, he did learn that the following night I was to play a lead role in a production of a show called *Another Yesterday* at Kirkdale Community Centre.

'You're not doing it, you're grounded,' he roared.

I couldn't let the show down at such short notice so I snuck out of the house and went anyway, petrified the whole time that he would walk into the hall and drag me off stage. When I got home, he battered me and threw me into bed.

But I had found something that I truly loved and I dread to think what I would have done if I had not been able to act. It wasn't just an escape outlet for me to survive. I think my teachers and the am-dram group could see I was more than capable too. I don't know how you stand out at the age of three but somebody obviously saw something because even then, I had been cast as Joseph in the school nativity.

Life can sometimes be a juggling act between what lies in your genetics and the path you choose to take and the effect those experiences have on you shape your character. Clearly, from the earliest possible moment, I was veering towards a stage.

Anything animated grabbed me. At my first nursery I had taken Googie, the famous Liverpool Duck, in to show everyone, complete with posters and the duck's hit single that had swept Merseyside. I realise you have probably never heard of it! The next day, for some reason, the nursery burnt down and all the contents were destroyed. Inside was Googie. On the inside, I was utterly heartbroken for weeks! To the outside world, I was already a big softie. I was the guy who mourned a dead duck, which was not even a real duck.

In time, the only place I would not get bullied was in the safety of the drama group. Beyond that, I was fair game and it was open season.

I *have* learnt to block it out over the years but that does not mean I have dealt with it. I still see many of the images today.

Dad told my sister after the first beating that she had to walk me home in future. Girl walks boy home. We used to have to trek across this field and one day it was absolutely belting down and I was attacked and left badly cut and bruised in the mud. They ragged my school jumper off me, which enraged Dad so much he sent me back to look for it. I found it soaking, stretched and full of holes in a puddle near the field. It was a senseless beating, but my classmates knew they could get away with it. I was just eight at the time.

In my third year at Senior School, I had left one lunchtime (which I always hated doing) to go to the shop. As I left the premises, a gang of about 30 or 40 lads surrounded me forming two lines in an arch, which they then made me walk through. As I did, the arch all but collapsed on me and then they piled in, kicking, spitting and urinating, throwing bricks and sticks at me. My blazer and school trousers were ruined and there was nothing I could do.

I did report it and told the head, Mr Wallace, that they had called me queer. His response was to send me home with a letter saying that I had been fighting.

I don't know why I was picked on. I can only assume that I was perceived as weak because I did 'girly things'. I did not understand words like anxiety and depression at that age, nor were they talked about, but the seeds were sewn. I used to spend hours in bed racking my brain for ways to avoid school, imagining throwing myself down the stairs, taking tablets or stepping out in front of a vehicle. From as young as eight these thoughts dominated my head, but I ultimately lacked the bottle. I couldn't bring myself to end it. I knew being hit by a bus was

10

likely to hurt, but my rationale was telling me that it wouldn't be as bad as the beatings. It was better to hurt my body than my feelings. How did I get to such a daft mind set? I didn't know the word suicide. I just wanted it over.

I wet the bed until I was fourteen. Mum had to change it every day and finally took me to the doctor who fed me some rubbish about needing to stretch my bladder but I knew why it was happening. I just went along with the GP who made me keep a chart and gave me gold stars if I went several nights without weeing.

I did cure it and that gave me the confidence to say yes to a school trip away at a dry ski slope in County Durham. We were gone a couple of nights and set up in bunks in our room. But I knew what was coming. I could always sense when a beating was due. My classmates would get rowdier and rowdier and one night took a pillow to my head to suffocate me. The teachers ignored it. My leg was too badly injured and the rest of my body was so grazed with cuts that I didn't get to ski much. I would never go on another school trip. I continued to sleep in my urine.

On one occasion I did try to take on the school bully – much to his annoyance. Revenge was soon forthcoming as he met me off the bus one day with his two brothers to absolutely annihilate me. They were waiting for me and broke my cheekbone.

When I got home, I just said that I was mugged. I had given up saying that I was attacked. It was pointless. I was forever making up excuses for those who went for *me* – a common symptom for people who are abused so regularly.

I had no logical explanation but it kept happening. I still did not understand at this point what gay was. I had never known this was the reason nor that I was. I would lie awake trying to work out what that isolating emotion was but I didn't understand it. I thought I was being bullied because of the way that I looked or acted. I could not blame it on being gay if I didn't know what it was.

11

One Sunday when I was fourteen something happened. I just moved in with my grandparents. In fact, it was more the case that I simply did not go home, and then gradually Mum brought my stuff over and I never really went back. I don't know if it was because I changed my bus route or this attempt to disappear, but I felt a cloud lift temporarily. My relationship with my Granddad (on my Mum's side) was better than with my own father. Sometimes, that can be the case, but we were able to talk about things that were taboo at home. Frankly, much had been off limits there.

With the move came the first steps to freedom. The bullying continued at school, but I didn't have to look over my shoulder. My teacher, Nicky Lindsay, who ran her own casting agency, also had a contract to supply extras for TV shows. So, on Thursday nights I was free to act and, if the opportunities came along, I no longer had to sneak out.

I have very fond memories of living there, from simple things like having money spent on shoes for the first time to seeing my first proper stage show, watching Cilla Black at the Empire Theatre, starring in *Aladdin,* but coming out on stage singing *Surprise Surprise,* as she did on TV. She was a role model to me – representing the girl from round here who had done good, and it was the first time I had seen a real star in a live production, and I knew I was born to do it. That Liverpool connection, and the pride that went with it, resonated with all of us too.

It gave me a spur and belief and soon extra work was coming in. I found myself playing a rent boy who frequented an arcade in Channel 4's *Brookside* in a role which lasted on and off for a year. Suddenly, it was real and I was dealing with professionals and sitting in the canteen around actors whom I had been watching on television for years. My Dad did learn about this – it was hard to hide – and, predictably, he flipped.

He didn't want me doing it at all. It was a no to drama and definitely that particular part and perhaps in his world another truth was hidden – that he knew I was gay and this was his one chance to have an outburst through the role of a *character* I was playing. Of course, many people in theatre were. He could see where this was heading.

But I carried on in the role and took other parts from a factory worker in war-torn Britain to walk-on parts in the teen soap, *Hollyoaks.* It was perfect. I was learning my trade amongst people I revered and I was getting paid for it. Most importantly, I think, I was fighting my demons. I hadn't yet said out loud that I was gay, but I knew that feeling of being different, and every time you took a part, a round of applause, or a pay cheque, somehow you were fighting back and rising above the tormentors. To a small audience in a playground they could be the Big I Am. On a stage, however small the role, I felt like a giant.

By the time I came to leave school at seventeen, I somehow managed to acquire five GCSEs, but I have never been more thrilled than to have walked out of there for the last time.

On many occasions since, I have gone back to Liverpool, past familiar landmarks, as if taking the school route again, and I still feel a shiver down my spine. I would do everything I possibly could to take an alternative route. Equally, to this day, when I see big gangs of lads or any kind of crowd, I turn the other way. If I do take the bus, I wait for everyone else to get on first so I can see that I am safe. I was naïve to think that leaving school would be the end of the abuse. It wasn't.

The bullying continued.

Chapter Two

When I stepped into the big wide world the harassment did not end, but it was easier to avoid.

I enrolled at Greenbank Performing Arts. I had no career plan, but looking back, it seemed to be the only outlet where I had expressed myself. I lasted six months before I had to give up. As much as I did not want to use public transport close to the places where I had been attacked, Greenbank itself was too far away and that was the reason I just couldn't keep commuting there.

At seventeen, I was left wondering what now? I had no money, few qualifications, hardly any friends and was living well within my soul because of the aggression towards me. The only time I had felt myself was when I was cut free to perform in the skin of other characters through drama. I understand now, if not then, that the assumption of and revelling in a fictional identity was a replacement for my own lack of self-worth.

I knew deep down that all I wanted to be was a Bluecoat. I had spent all those summer holidays at Pontins in Blackpool – an old school British holiday by the seaside, *but* one where there was wall to wall entertainment. Whilst everyone else was taking a donkey ride or waiting for the sun to come out, I just followed the bright lights in awe of those who put on show after show, whilst also doubling up as athletes for a relentless sporting programme. I knew that this was what I wanted to do.

There was only one problem. You had to be eighteen.
So I lied.
And even though I was one year short, I was accepted.

All roads led to Torquay. At my interview, I had to state where I wanted to work and you were given three options, so I wrote Blackpool and nothing else and then I got the call saying that I had got the job. I was heading to the English Riviera – which was not Blackpool.

I now faced several challenges.

Geographically, I did not have a clue where I was heading. It felt as though it might have been as far away as America. I arrived to palm trees and thought it was Spain and the train took forever to get there, passing more fields and trees than a lad from Liverpool could ever imagine.

But I felt good, if a little looking over my shoulder. My limited am-dram experience had got me to interview. Some singing and role-playing meant I passed that stage. Nobody checked my age. I hoped that they would not spot that I was out of my depth. More importantly, I was so far away from the horrors of growing up in Liverpool with the bullying, that I felt as though I had been given a new chance. I had everything to live for.

I loved the visiting cabaret acts. I recognised that these people knew their craft. Turns likes Susanne Maud, nailing the classic *Bobby's Girl* every single time, filled me with awe. She was the Jane McDonald of her day.

The late Caroline Aherne, famous for the TV show *The Royle Family* and *Mrs Merton* also came to film a segment for the travel programme, *Wish You Were Here,* with her then husband, Peter Hook from the band, *New Order,* and I watched in awe as she effortlessly and naturally had everyone in hysterics. She gave me my first TV appearance. I was in amongst my type of people and in awe of them, but finding that confidence and self-expression that had been lacking beyond the early extra work. I know that I was starting to find myself because I dyed my hair blonde. It was fun but gruelling – the work, not the colouring!

I lasted nine months and my God it was draining. Two hours of sneaking out to do am dram behind my Dad's back once a week was nothing compared to an endless trawl of a six-day week that began at seven to say good morning to everyone breakfasting and ended way past midnight the next day.

Who on holiday needs their first cooked meal at the crack of dawn and why was it so important that the Bluecoats were up to greet them…just to say 'good morning'?

It was relentless – non-stop, featuring hourly sessions of quizzes and bowls in the morning and afternoons of netball and donkey races, finishing at 4 pm, but never stopping, because you had to do 'dinner doors', welcoming people into tea and then, after your own meal, getting ready for the show at 9! It didn't stop there. After the show, you might be assigned the club or the room with the live band. These could finish anywhere between 1 and 3 am. You were relieved if you got the live band and could finish a couple of hours earlier than the disco!

When we weren't working in each other's faces, we were living in each other's pockets. I would tire of the double standards of the Entertainment Manager having sex all night and keeping us awake in the tiny window that we had to sleep before it was time to get up again at 6 am.

Staff turnover was high – they were always recruiting, and there was a hierarchy. Some people lasted a day and couldn't hack it. Others were looking to move up all the time and work their way to the job of that all-powerful Entertainments Manager. You could be working with someone one day and never see them again. Equally, you could be looking for your cues in a show and find that a new recruit was in the role. It was tough, and by June 1995 I had had enough and they had of me. I tried too hard to get on with people. I knew I was doing this but I desperately wanted to be liked in my new-found freedom. The bullying had at least stopped, but I was binned and at less than £90 a week, I wouldn't really miss it.

But, it was a good grounding. Nor did I feel anything negative about Pontins – far from it. It had been one of the best things I had ever done and I had begun to find myself. I also knew that back then this was where it all started. So many people whom I admired had started this way, and I felt the door remained very much open. This was the route to the cruise ships and the much sought-after Equity Card.

As I made my way back to Liverpool, I could not have imagined that my Granddad was about to play a major role in my career.

Chapter Three

I had signed on the dole for two months, getting my Giro but thinking I was a millionaire. I always needed to chase the next thing, but was tired and had almost zero inclination to pursue the dream right now. But it didn't matter. Those aspirations were about to be placed on hold.

It is now early August 1995 and out of the blue we got a call to say my beloved Granddad had been taken to hospital. None of us had seen it coming and were not overly concerned, so we packed up sandwiches and made our way in and found him fine.

He was chatting away. I handed him the newspaper and we laughed about the main story of Michael Barrymore, who had announced that he was finally coming out. We both loved him and watched all his shows. He, too, had been a Bluecoat.

'I think I am gay,' I confessed to Granddad – words I could never say to my Dad.

'I know you are,' he replied.

I could not be the first person who had been building up to this kind of announcement only to blurt it out to almost no reaction. And that was it. Done in an instant.

'Be what you wanna be,' he told me.

And he never spoke again.

Over the years I would hear his words in my head on countless occasions. They became my mantra.

I told Nanna what I had confessed to Granddad and she said she knew too. It was never mentioned after that.

We had left him overnight after the nurses had said he would probably be fine in the morning. He wasn't.

He died that night.

I had woken in the early hours with a horrible sickly feeling in my stomach – one like I had never experienced before. I looked at my watch and it had stopped at 0550. Meanwhile, Nanna had taken a call to go back in, but was too late. He had died of a heart attack on a foot ward with no resuscitation unit to hand at the exact time my watch had packed up.

I was devastated. If anything, I was closer to my grandparents than my own. They had been the steadying calm of acceptance during the bullying teens when Dad would go mad if I went to drama. They took me in and facilitated my aspirations in that field. They really had given me a start from nowhere and now I felt like my world had collapsed. When I say that nothing would be the same again, it is not a cliché, because I still feel that today about him and wish that he had been with me on the 'journey' that was to come. He had certainly given me the start and freed me from the pressure of parents. Awkward family life had become a pleasure just sitting around watching TV and having tea, without fearing I would put a foot out of place. The truth is that half the people I knew in Liverpool had been brought up by their Nan and Granddad.

Anxiety that had begun with the bullying kicked in again, and those simple things in life in the short term were beyond me. From the moment we lost him, I was unable to shower or eat and cried constantly. I carried myself in a trance state – a haze of sadness shadowing me. I watched my Nan, a strong woman, fall distraught and constantly breaking down.

Then came the funeral – the longest and hardest of days. I was in no fit state to perform any kind of duties, and the weight of carrying Granddad was in every sense physical and mental. We were so distraught that we tried to stop the hearse taking the coffin away. I was unable to deliver a speech I had written, replaced instead by a song I had recorded a few years before after winning a competition. Every family has these personal compartments in their lockers and this song was mine and Granddad's.

Afterwards, everywhere I went reminded me of him. The memories were constant. It took until the *X Factor* to get over him and I am not even sure that is the case – more like managing the pain. It was the suddenness of his death that destroyed me. Everybody knows that feeling when they wished

20

they could have a final conversation or turn back the clock, but in the movie in your mind, the scene gets stuck where you are having that conversation about Michael Barrymore, and you tell him you will be back tomorrow, but then there is no fresh morning…just mourning of a different kind.

I was totally at a loss, skint on the dole, without direction and now deprived of the most important male influence in my life. I didn't know what to do. I was broken.

Chapter Four

I was thrown a lifeline. Pontins were back in touch. They were recruiting specifically for Blackpool and obviously knew that I had left Torquay. Blackpool was always where I wanted to be. As far as I was concerned, Torquay was B list in comparison for the career…and so far away from home.

But I was stunned that they had called – and by the timing.

They knew me at Blackpool too, not just because of the work I had done at Torquay, but because every summer we had been there on holiday I had besieged all the talent competitions, winning every year. So, I was both an ex-employee and a known quantity to them.

We chatted about Torquay and why I had to leave and they said that the company would like to use me somewhere else.

'Thanks for the call,' I wrapped up and began to feel the first major mood change for the better since Granddad had died. It had only been four weeks.

'There's a lot going on at the moment,' I stalled. 'Can I give you a call in about a week?

It *was* Blackpool – where I had always wanted to be, and yet I was not exactly charging towards it. My head was mashed and I needed someone to tell me what to do and that person had gone.

I had no choice but to ask Nanna what she thought, even though that meant leaving her on her own. She could see that I had just been sat around moping and having far too much to drink on the sly that I had to go…and of course, they wanted me yesterday because someone had left and they needed me to walk straight into the part. So, finally I agreed and, in no time at all, was back, dressing up in fancy costumes again and once more being largely assigned the effeminate parts.

But it was a mistake. Professionally, it was a new beginning, but emotionally I was not ready, still with the haze of grief hanging over me and my eyes were permanently sunken from all the tears I shed back at the chalet after performances. I was back on the treadmill way too soon. Activities – tears – performance – tears – sleep – repeat. The only smiles were for the public.

It was Torquay all over again in terms of routine, but with the grief and for the saving grace that I was now having much more to do with the shows. In a way, without gaining a title in the Pontins hierarchy, which I did not particularly crave, except that it showed you were progressing and climbing up the ladder towards recognition. It was a massive thumbs-up for me, and even though I had left Torquay, Blackpool saw something that they trusted and could nurture.

I think that it was horses for courses as well. The staff turnaround was still high – entertainers always wanted the next rung. If they could make me happy by allowing the responsibility of contributing, rather than just being a smiley gob on a stick who said good morning at breakfast and thank you and goodnight at the end of a show, then it suited everybody. They knew I wouldn't come back to be a dogsbody and I was well aware that this was the gateway to the cruise ships.

So, in between grief, I threw myself at a *La Bamba* show and the classic standard of *The Magical of the Musicals,* a variety show featuring snippets of all the big productions that you see all around the world. This time it was proper entertainment. If you wander down the front at Blackpool, it can look tacky and traditional in a dated way, but make no mistake there are thousands of professionals there working long hours, plying their trade and vying for your business, along a coastline where there are many options. That alone made it stand out from Torquay. There were also simpler, subtler improvements. The stage and the staging were a different level of professionalism, and I was now playing an auditorium rather than a mere dance floor.

It *was* a good move. It was definitely the right thing to do. It just came at the lowest point of my life. But maybe timing was everything, I became a mixture of full-on professionalism to staff and audiences, but once alone, a personal disaster. Of course, the performing helped me block out the grief and like everyone in this situation, you have to get back on the horse at some point. Even though nobody can ever see it at the time, life does go on.

I *did* begin to feel a little better but there was not one day when I didn't rest my grief. Under the spotlight though, I found a way of being *on it* and raising my game. This was – they say – the Vegas of the North! My confidence generally began to return and on stage it soared. I was also around a different level of professionalism. It felt great that, in my eyes, Woody, the Entertainments Manager, came across as quite jealous to some of the acclaim that I was starting to gain. In short, it was very competitive amongst the talent and all the bookers.

It turned out that it was an old friend, Jackie, who had recommended me. Jack was already in a show, and was ahead of me in terms of the game. One night she told me that Roger was in. I knew this would drive my Ents Manager potty. More importantly, Roger had come to see me and this was the big one. You only got one chance to make a first impression.

Roger is Roger Kendrick. He was the man. Jackie thought Rog was coming to see her and she thought this was *her* moment. I owe her for getting me back in, but Roger told me after that he had seen my vocals, stage presence, and charisma in *The Magic of the Musicals* and that he was blown away. Would I like to work for him?

He too had stage presence. Everybody knew he was the connection to the cruise ships. He could make you or break you on his say so, and his image radiated just that – I remember him coming in with his big glasses, dressed almost Mafioso. I had never really met an agent before, but he owned it from the start!

He took my number and true to his word, did call. That, in itself, was a massive boost. There is a reason that the phrase

'I'll call you' is much parodied – principally because when someone says it, that generally means they won't. But he did.

When he rang, we talked and talked and he kept telling me I was going to be fab and *it* was going to be amazing, but then... nothing. He did not offer me a job. I was stunned, but it was an early lesson in this business that when you think you are in, you never really are and only when it is signed and sealed does it become delivered, and even then, fame and fortune are fickle and the next hot shot comes along or there is a whiff of negativity and you are out.

So, I put the phone down perplexed thinking maybe I had blown it, but at least the contact was made. Jackie did not get that call. I could not sit around wondering, and of course, I know now how these things work. That first conversation was a test to see how badly I wanted it and if my character was strong enough to survive. If you like, it only prepares you for what goes on in the TV talent show process. He knew what I could do because he had seen me live. But he didn't *know* me and if I had it in me.

When nothing happened for a couple of weeks, it began to play on my mind. I was so desperate and perhaps being grief-stricken did not make me at my most pro-active, but I kept re-visiting the conversation in my head and somehow found the energy to do something about it.

When I was fifteen, I had been to see Joe Longthorne perform in Southport and absolutely loved his act. I was old school in that I adored variety. I did not see why sometimes it had become a dirty word. To me, it just said that you were very good at lots of things. I was fortunate enough to meet Joe and he was kind enough to grant me his time. I told him that I wanted to become a singer and as a lot of people do in this situation, he said that if I was ever in Blackpool, to get in touch. Most people did not mean it. It was a way of palming you off.

But, in a rare moment of courage amidst the darkness around me, I had nothing to lose. I bit the bullet and called his manager Basil, and sure enough, they both turned up at one of my shows. Joe was a hero to me, so this was big pressure, hugely flattering and again – a rare example of a decent human being true to his word.

Or maybe that isn't quite the truth. I met Basil after and he told me to come and see him at his bedsit in Blackpool. I explained that I had spoken with Roger, but nothing had happened and would it be possible for him to put a good word in for me. I had my reservations, but when I turned up, he assured me that he would.

He then made a pass at me. I still didn't know that I was definitely gay at this point. Either way, my Gaydar seemed to be up and running and was registering warning signs. It all suddenly seemed very seedy to me, and thoughts of sleeping your way to the top suddenly went from being a cliché to feeling scarily real.

The daft thing is that when I made my excuses and left, Roger did call a few days later. There can be no explanation for that sequence of events. Maybe Basil did put in a word in the hope that I might then offer him 'thanks' or perhaps he just did anyway because he thought I had something. Or possibly Roger *just* called. If I have learnt one thing about being an overnight success, it is that it takes time! It is quite likely that Roger phoned when it suited him and when he had an opportunity. Even though your life and your career are all consuming for you yourself, I was yet to learn that *you* are part of a process – one name of many on an agent's books and never ever his only client.

But he *did* ring and I was offered a six-month contract at sea. I said yes instantly even though I did not want to go physically. I was far from ready and it was far from home. But I had to pull myself together fast. This is what I had been working for and waiting on for years. The cruise ship was the dream. In the years ahead, it had become a talent show put-down, a derogatory snide comment that said you were good enough for a certain audience but not really for anything beyond that, but I did not know that at the time and nor did I ever see it that way. I viewed it as an endless opportunity and –

make no mistake – another gruelling schedule of live work with a captive audience who couldn't get off the boat and would want performances that were not the *repeat* of the night before. I respected its discipline, work ethic and career path. From here I could always jump ship – so to speak – and go to the next level after this.

But of course, it was a massive step. I was literally all at sea as I said yes to the Mediterranean and bye to Nanna, worrying constantly that she would not be OK without me there. Plus – I was still dealing with my own demons and I could not have imagined how depressed I was at Granddad's passing. Death happens to us all, but it was the fact that one minute my rock was there and the next he was gone. I had no time to prepare myself for it and was misled that his passing away was unlikely the night we left him. That must have contributed to the lingering delayed shock, living on autopilot.

I was drifting. I had been in Blackpool two months. Somehow, I had agreed to go but the thing that meant the most to me outside my family had suddenly meant the least. I did not envisage leaving Blackpool so soon and in a town where the next offer is often the best offer, loyalty is at a premium. So, when I approached my boss, Woody, he had already got wind. To me, he seemed like a parody caricature with his Brummie accent and blonde mullet as he fired me on the spot – just for being tapped up.

At times, the entertainment industry seemed to operate by its own rules, regardless of the law. It meant I left the North West with my eyes wide open as to the way this business worked – seediness, to those promising they would call, to those who were actually true to their word.

I loved Blackpool – for its childhood memories and endless opportunity, but I was delighted to leave this boss too, even though my head was not entirely in the best place.

By October, I was rehearsing. In December, I joined the ship and, by this point, I was beginning to believe again that once you have done a cruise, you can do anything. A singer on a cruise ship *was* the best job in the world. I was still low, probably not ready and definitely drinking too much, but I could walk that line between professional me and personal me, and yes, I did still want it and, in my moments of a clearer rationale, knew I had to do it. Sometimes I had the clarity to realise that for a lad from a council estate in Liverpool to do this was massive. I knew that deep down, just as I was aware that if I rejected Roger once, I would not be asked twice.

It still did not stop me breaking down the night before I left, crying my eyes out at Nanna's. I felt terrible for leaving her – my grandparents had given me the only security I had known. They were at the beginning of the process where I started to find the real me. With a heavy heart, it was time to go. Ahead, lay opportunity and more self-discovery. My dream was on. Where most people look to London for the bright lights, my head turned in another direction. I was staring out to sea.

Chapter Five

What on earth was I thinking? I had never even been on a plane before, let alone make a boat on the ocean my new home. My dreams had taken over. I had no idea what to expect, but I believed it was going to be amazing. What I felt in nerves at the airport was met equally in excitement. But this was it.

I was greeted by a couple of dancers, and two seasoned old pros, in Jez and Donna, the resident musicians. They must have laughed at my naivety. It was another flight, another ocean and another season for them. I sat at the back of the plane on the way out chain-smoking, in the days when you still could.

We were straight into two weeks of rehearsals, given our songs to learn and told to get on with it. I took the lead vocals at the age of seventeen.

The Red Sea, Oman, Egypt and Jordan beckoned. We were performers with no input and were expected to deliver four main shows a week, but that also meant you were assigned to run aqua aerobics and play classic cruise ship games, from bingo to quoits, keeping the mostly old and non-English speaking clientele content on this Greek vessel, in between the sunshine and next overdose of food. Expectations for our entertainment were not what they are today. If you could hold the song and things went more or less to plan then they were happy. Nowadays things have gone a lot more Disney.

The entertainment was not necessarily what I would have put on, but at this stage in my career, I was just grateful for the work, so I threw myself at *Songs From Around the World* and *Arabian Nights,* and the customary *Crew Show,* and generally found it less professional than Blackpool, where the talent was used to churning shows and there was plenty of choice – your competitors were often right next door. In the middle of the ocean, you were it.

I kept telling myself it was an incredible opportunity, that this was the career route and I would learn a lot. The first basic rule, of course, is that whatever the arena and whoever the audience, you must put your heart and soul into it regardless. And I did.

But just like Blackpool, I found the lows in between performances a little hard to manage, though there was at least the wonder of seeing a little bit of the world. I didn't get bored of circling the ocean and thinking that if it were Wednesday then it must be Israel. I was not a seasoned enough hand yet to succumb to the monotony of the ocean. In fact, I did want to explore and positively loved seeing the dolphins in and I used to look forward to jumping ashore for bargains at prices I could only dream of back home.

It was a culture shock though for sure. A lad with my upbringing was probably not ready for the Arab world. I know I stared a lot as they probably did at me. Their customs and demeanour were a completely new culture. Of course, I knew that a world like this existed. At times I marvelled, and at others, I felt lost with it, and so far away from home.

And of course, working the cruise ships radiated glamour in people's minds – what a life and a chance to see the world in constant sunshine and be fed and watered. The reality was a little different.

In the late 1990s, food aboard was rationed – you would largely eat with the multi-national crew of Greek, Spanish, Italian and just a few of us English. You were supposed to be limited to a couple of drinks and then you retired to the bowels of the ship, cooped up in a bunk bed that was barely able to accommodate a tall person. When you hit the lows and wandered back to your cabin in the middle of the night, with barely a soul you knew around, well aware that you had to do it all again the next day, then sometimes you literally could hit rock bottom.

On stage I came alive but off it, as much as Jez and Donna looked after me and kept me going, I know I came across as young and visibly nervous. Back in the cabin, that anxiety returned.

I lasted eight weeks.

Shafted at sea.

From the second week in rehearsals, I began to feel intimidating stares. The eyes of the Chief Engineer, a slimy 40-something Greek with weird, horrible, murderous eyes never left me. I felt his gaze in the back of my head and wherever I turned in the maze of the vessel, I always seemed to run into him. I was literally stalked out to sea.

At the standard safety drills, he would pick on me and just stand there giving me horrible looks. Generally, he would grunt at me and only speak in English if I got a question wrong.

I know I came across as slightly flamboyant and quite artistic – a typical luvvie perhaps, and in my naivety, assumed that this was a culture shock for him too. It wasn't. He had other plans.

One night, he came to my cabin. He shouldn't have even been on my floor. I had no light either and at night I could just make out a crack through the door. Then it widened, waking me from my sleep.

I smelt whisky on his breath and spotted his white overalls, silhouetting against the darkness. Then he pulled my pyjama bottoms down and began to thrust his way towards me. I had had no sexual experience.

I don't know if he came to punish me from his position of power amongst the crew or if his behaviour previously was hiding some sort of crush. Either way, he was drunk and it was vile. As I pushed him off, he began to attack me, punching me as I resisted, attempting to put his hand on my mouth. I felt sick.

I screamed for England and broke the stillness that you always found in the bottom of the ship. He had no choice but to flee. He was caught a few minutes later turning the corner of a floor, peddling the line that he had in fact been doing a late-night security walk round. Jez and Donna had heard my screams and knew me well enough in just a handful of weeks to see that I was not bluffing.

It was all over in five minutes. Jez and Donna had seen it all before – the cultural differences covering up chauvinism and abuse of power amongst the hierarchy of a home crew. It was a sinister and underhand clique. Despite manning the vessel, many of the senior operatives were drinking most nights, long before proper checks came in.

In the moment, it probably did seem an unlikely event but looking back, they knew how coarse he was, singling me out for special treatment. One of the problems of being bullied at school is that if this is largely all you know, so when it happens in a new set of circumstances, you just see it as the norm and your level of acceptance plateaus. You do not fight because you do not see anything different from before. Only the environment has changed. That is the effect of abuse, and control. The victim is blind and muted.

The next day we were both asked to do a full report into what happened. He, a staff member would submit his to his boss. Myself, contracted for a six-month spell, would do the same. I knew how this was going.

Petrified, I didn't leave the cabin for 24 hours. I just lay there listening to music. Jez and Donna fed me. I didn't perform that night. I fell foul to the jurisdiction of the sea…

Two days later, I was told that I was leaving and that the officer would be transferring to another ship. It is hard to imagine that this was an isolated incident. I would be told to disembark at Eilat in Israel. I saw no reason why it should be me other than the fact that it just seemed to be my fate.

The process was brutal, let alone unjust. Two guards came to my cabin to watch me pack and oversee that I wasn't stealing anything from this most barren of environments where there was nothing to pinch. At 6 am as we docked, I was first off the ship to tears from Jez and Donna. I broke down as I said my farewells. Bar three of the team, I would never see any of them again, and when I later did meet Jez and Donna they confirmed that in fact the engineer had remained on board. The conspiracy of silence was deafening.

Now, I panicked. I was abandoned portside and had to wait several hours for the staff on the dock to process me and that meant a 20-seater aircraft from Eilat to Tel Aviv. I had no idea where I was or how I was getting home. I had $100 in my wallet. Nor did I have any way of contacting anyone. On the ship, you had to buy a card and ring from reception. The signal was poor and it was expensive. On dry land and out of funds, I couldn't make that call. Nor did I know what to say.

The journey from hell had begun, running into an appalling winter and Christmas chaos back home, I was delayed and forced to stay overnight in Tel Aviv, then shunted on a flight to Gatwick, still miles from home, forcing me to change the dollars and shell out what was left on a National Express back to Liverpool, which added another twelve hours to the journey.

I was devastated and at a new low. Christmas and the cold emphasised the solitude. Nobody wanted to return with their tail between their legs. I didn't want to have to recount the story.

When I turned up unexpected I just said that the management company had lost the contract and we had been terminated early. I lied to spare my blushes. The situation was simple. I had no money and was freezing. I worked myself into such a state that I needed a doctor's note to avoid becoming a permanent nervous wreck. That attack left scars that would never heal.

Chapter Six

In the New Year, the dust settled a little. That pressure of Christmas was removed and the low that had been accentuated by not at all feeling festive levelled out. It was January and *everyone* was fed up.

I called the management company who had sent me out there as I was still owed $1000 and desperately wanted to work. It was not my fault in any way that I was now home. I got short changed – and indeed no change.

They refused to acknowledge what had happened, so desperate were they to cling to all the cruise ship contracts. I never got a penny back, fobbed off with the line that the money had been swallowed up getting me home.

As I left the ship I was threatened that I would never work a cruise ever again. The management company insinuated the same. Despite the start in my career that it gave me, it was not worth it at all.

As I write this in 2018, the world has more rounded views to mental health, sexual abuse, exploitation in the work place and the general behaviour in the past of some in entertainment, who abused their power and considered themselves exempt from the rules of society. But this is exactly the cover-up mentality that did exist and is now being exposed. To speak out meant you probably wouldn't work again. To this day, it churns my stomach in knots.

Of course, I believed this too. Only now that I have seen and heard these threats first hand or to other people do I fully understand the game and refuse to be intimidated by it.

Then, it was a different story and I took it at its word. All I wanted to do was sing. I was resigned to the fact that it was over and I needed money. I headed for work in a call centre.

By chance, I learned of the newspaper, *The Stage,* which was the bible for all sorts of acting work. One day I spotted an ad for a lead singer on the Stena Sealine from

Southampton to Cherbourg in France. With nothing to lose, I applied. Suddenly, I was back in the game.

I got the job as resident singer on the booze cruise, back in the basement again and performing once a day for a bunch of bargain-hunting pissed up Brits. They didn't board the ferry to watch me, but it was the perfect chance to hone my craft a little more. I didn't see dry land for weeks. Life consisted of the monotonous channel hop, dock, sleep and then back again.

It was a downgrade for sure – but it was work. I used to mis-refer to it amongst my colleagues and they would set me straight.

'It's a cross channel ferry, not a cruise,' they would say.

And they were right.

Five hours and the rabble were off. You weren't stuck with them for two weeks! Every time though that I now took to sea, Israel flashed back to haunt me. The confined space, the control asserted and the attempted assault filled me with panic each time I thought about it.

But there was one glimmer of hope.

I met Nigel.

Chapter Seven

My first love was waiting on tables in the buffet section. He was also waiting for me. I used to find a way to go up above to the passenger area and see him from my grim bunker underneath. I was just drawn to him and that meant you made excuses. Suddenly food became a priority!

I was not supposed to venture up there – the Ents team and the public were to be kept well apart! But once we caught each other's eyes, it became inevitable. It is very difficult to express. I had told Granddad on his deathbed I was gay. But there hadn't actually been any proof. I had been all but assaulted on the first cruise. But I had never yet met a man. I felt instantly attracted to him. It was a light bulb moment and it shone brightly.

A few days after I first saw him there was an unofficial crew party and we were sharing *Foster's* beer. We left together and that different feeling that I had always felt but been unable to express was starting to surface. Nigel escorted me to my cabin but fell short of coming in. He kissed me goodnight and I knew. That was what was missing.

Within a couple of days, the grim routine life in a cabin under the sea was transformed. Nigel all but moved in and we were decorating the tiny space like it was our first love nest. My room had a bunk bed, a table and chair and Nigel took the bottom bunk. Somehow, we made it fit and work. I had found myself and we were blissfully happy.

Of course, I knew no different and I thought this was it. It was one thing to discover what I think I already knew and then another to express myself openly and embrace the relationship. I hadn't known what I was missing. But now I did.

When my six-month contract came to an end across the channel, I was keen to continue, but abandoned it all for the relationship. We had agreed to move in together.

We spent the last night on board as one and I took a taxi from Southampton to Portsmouth to his flat, knowing this was it.

I knocked on the door to discover that he was living with Pollyanna.

'I'm sorry I can't,' he announced.

'But I've made all my plans,' I pleaded.

'I know, I can't.'

He dumped me.

I had never been in a relationship. I gave it all up to be with him. Now, I was not in a relationship. I had crashed and burned in an instant. I had never felt one to one rejection – just permanently as a theme in my life.

I know now it was a superficial summer romance and I understand that I place attention to it because it was my first, but I was clueless and hopeless. I had made my plans to settle in Hampshire and instead found myself back on any train that would take me home. When I got there, I ripped up all our pictures like a jealous lover, though, years later, when I matured, I did find the negatives and got them re-printed because they were essentially happy times.

I had proved so much to myself – that I could live away from home; that I had a great vocal; and most importantly, that Nigel had helped me find my identity.

At the time, I hated it, but it made me turn a corner that I did not know was there. I hold only fond memories and Nigel came to see me in panto in 2013 where I was devastated to learn that he had been quite poorly. You never know what hand fate will deal you.

His legacy to me though is my sexuality. The penny had dropped. Everything I was missing now slotted into place like a jigsaw puzzle. Gutted at Nigel and I biting the dust, I was mostly relieved, overwhelmed and euphoric that I had found myself.

I had nothing to go back to Liverpool to, but at least my own personal journey had begun.

Chapter Eight

I had no boyfriend, no job and no purpose – but finally I knew who I was. I was temping for Liverpool Mutual Homes. I had gone from singing to dealing with rent arrears, anti-social behaviour and windows being boarded up.

I sold car insurance, dealt with cold callers and debt collection issues. I was very lenient because I knew that many people calling me were on the dole and really could not afford repayments. So, I would chat all the time, exchanging life stories. Rather than resolving issues for the council, I would just try to make people happy. Inside, with my headphones on, all I wanted to do was sing. I only killed the call when the red light went and my time was up.

I loved making a difference.

But soon I got a job back on the cruises. I was assigned to the *Topaz.* A pattern was developing. I did not last long. One rocky night, I was making my way back to my cabin with almost no lights. Trying to find my way around, I smashed my right hand into the glass area where my toothbrush was.

It was critical. I had damaged the main artery in my right hand and lost a significant amount of blood.

Packed off to see the doctor, I lay on the operating table, dripping blood everywhere. As they operated on me, I could see everything they were doing. It was like an out of body experience, except that I was living it for real.

I woke an hour later. My hand was still bleeding. I was told that I had died. Furthermore, if I did not leave the ship at Santa Cruz, Tenerife, I would probably lose my hand. I turned away as they numbed it. I did not want to lose it. At worst, I needed to hold a microphone. They just about strapped it together.

My tendons were cut. The ligaments and muscles were all gone. I had no sensation in the hand. The surgeons had to go inside my arm to put me back together. It was close to the worst physical experience that I had ever experienced.

I had to quit obviously but was fortunate enough to get a job with *First Choice*. This time, I lasted five months. I found out my uncle had advanced multiple sclerosis whilst I was at sea. He was at a very advanced stage and I asked to go home for just a day to see him. On the Monday, he was fine. By the weekend, he was in a wheelchair. The company said no. So, I quit, borrowing the money to fly home.

I took a job in the USA. I think my head was ripped between wanting to be at home near Nan and Mum and its safety net, but getting twitchy feet to perform and that, whether home or abroad, would always mean travelling. It was something I had to conquer.

So, I would scour the publications again and daydream a little in between answering the calls in the call centre. I enjoyed chatting, I took great satisfaction in resolving problems and helping people, I liked being a Scouser amongst Scousers. But one thing remained: I had a taste of the business.

I cannot say that I had sampled the big time by any means, but I could see the path there and something was nagging at me that the one thing I had been sure of in life, when my own sexuality created such doubt in my interaction with people, was that I could perform and would be happy doing so.

I had also briefly met a guy called Gary and there was a spark, *yet* I had to pursue my dream. I knew I had to leave Liverpool again. I was keen on seeing him and I never stopped wondering about him.

I did not consider myself lucky. Experiences on the ships had reinforced that, but one day I was astonished to get a call out of the blue from a company who had just been looking online for talent and found a clip of me on *YouTube*. Would I like to come out to the States and work the cruises there? Was I available?

Wow – this was something else? Not only was I sent on one of the best gigs going – a ship from Fort Lauderdale to Columbia, Argentina, Venezuela, British Virgin Islands and Antigua *but* I had been spotted. I joked to myself that they must be desperate, yet they were one of the hardest companies to get work with. I gave myself a good talking to and that in fact I needed to believe again. The problem was that I sort of did and I sort of didn't.

I sat down with my bosses and told them I was off to see the world and was going to be famous and, as ever, they were gentlemanly in their acceptance. We both knew I would probably return.

I sold my furniture and gave up my flat. It was time to go.

So now I am off the coast of Florida and this time I have passenger status as an employee, which means I eat better and do not live in a bunker, though I did have to share a cabin. The Americans generally were much more big time and as anyone who has been to Disney knows, they invest in entertainment, where other countries and brands often cut corners. I also loved America and the more superficial easy-going nature of people.

I was nervous – and that emotion was heightened by what happened on that first cruise. Every time I had been away, I had always come home early. My track record was not great. This time I began to make friends. And also, one or two enemies.

Strangely it was one of my own who took a dislike to me. Janette Galbraith was from Liverpool and whilst that drew us together initially, it helped drive a competitive wedge between us. Sometimes in these claustrophobic environments you can believe you are friends with somebody and it is very easy to begin a bond with something as simple as recognising a similar accent. Unfortunately, professional jealousy can raise its ugly head and can reveal how flimsy the relationship is.

I turned up, glad to be performing again and in better a condition. That was my agenda. I wasn't looking to be the best. I just wanted to be. I knew if I was good then the work would speak for itself. I did not need to trample on any toes. If I delivered, I could get spotted again. One thing you always knew about a cruise ship was that there was generally money in the clientele. The audience seemed older and wiser too. They were also definitely more mature, which meant if they were still working people they could hold senior positions. But, you knew that you *never* knew who was in the audience, so being hired through *YouTube* could very much happen again. I was building a reputation.

In no time, I got my own show with a live band performing big songs like *Delilah* and *I Dreamed a Dream* and even the multi-nationals would join in with the 'Why why why…?'.

I was happy, content abroad in my own sexuality and, for once, not homesick. I loved Americana and the promotion of everything. The audience seemed to adore me. That meant more profile, more chance to stand out as an individual and 80 Euros a day rather than being paid monthly. A hierarchy existed on the ocean and I left her sailing behind at a speed of knots. I could do my own thing and that meant creative freedom, better pay and a chance to shine.

For once, I completed the contract. That would not be the last I heard of Janette Galbraith. You can probably guess at what point she would re-surface later and none of it was good. Her wild imagination, coupled with some dated photos were an opportunity too good for her to miss and something that had clearly been stored up in her sub-conscience from not long after we met. Our paths would cross again when the moment was right for her.

After America, I returned home, very satisfied and happy but still without genuine direction. I obviously could not sit around waiting for the phone to ring, although of course that was the obvious route back into work via the call centre in Liverpool. So, I temped again for Sefton Council but this time more than ever and probably because the American contract had been a success, I missed singing so much.

I think one of the key elements of that cruise was that I got spotted initially but then also was promoted on board. I was valued. Twice. Generally, you sign a deal and that is your gig for the duration. It really is only going to change if

44

somebody is poorly or leaves. Yet, somebody was taking me seriously in the entertainments division and was looking to better their act, and I benefitted within the contract. That, and the fact that I stayed the course gave me a high…which inevitably created a low.

It somehow was on a new level and that gave me something to cling to, yet the more phones I answered for the council, the less my own would ring with the next offer. I got such a buzz out of this trip and had not come home embarrassed, humiliated or compromised that it created a new pedestal, and whilst I will never belittle the call centre work and was grateful for their flexibility on many occasions, it left a void. And I needed to fill it.

I worked hard by day for twelve months. By night I hit the bars and drank too much again. I was plunging into a severe depression. I went for a permanent role at work and they knocked me back for the first time. Maybe it was a sign, an early shooting star. I had always had work there but I was falling apart at night. I couldn't see it at the time, of course. I was in a never-ending cycle, which was about to get worse. Next, they didn't renew my contract at all.

Suddenly, I had no job, no money, no partner, no career and I couldn't pay my bills. I had nothing and my heart was empty.

One night at my Mums, I drank more than normal and started scouring the place for medication. Like an alcoholic searching every cupboard for that last drink, I was looking for anything. I had voices inside my head and anxiety levels at an all time high. I could see little release. There was no escape.

I felt alone and the road ahead seemed bleak. Even though, I knew my parents did love me and my Nan and Granddad had been everything to me, something kicked in inside that meant that my mind was almost separated from my body, and that rational thoughts were a thing of the past. I talked myself into such a drunken state that the people I loved had become just characters over the horizon and that was a distance too far way. I couldn't reach out to them any more.

There were too many dark clouds. I had lost faith that even those who loved me couldn't help any more. I knew they cared – that was never in doubt – but my own mind had gone walkabout into a last chance saloon and, behind me, I had closed every door. As I lunged forward into a cloudy darkness, I could not see or touch what I was leaving behind. My mind was on loan to the devil.

I took everything. I had no idea what. It wasn't planned or researched, but it had been building. Now, I understand it was a cry for help. Then, I wasn't processing thoughts. I was not seeking a reaction. I was just looking for an escape. An end was all I craved.

I shoved every pill going in my mouth and tried to run out of the house. My legs caved in and I hit the floor. I remember nothing else until I woke in the Royal Hospital in Liverpool. My stomach had been pumped and all I could taste was charcoal. I know now that Mum called an ambulance. I am embarrassed that it happened in front of her. Only she really knows what I took and what happened in these missing hours.

When I came around, my Nan and sister were there. They probably had no idea about this true fight within me, except that they knew I had struggled with life. It is always the way that because you are alive and people see your ups and downs, they can never quite envisage the worst-case scenario, because you are still there every day and it is only a blip to them. They are not riding the same train as you. They can get off. They do not hear the silent words or the unexpressed torment in your head. It is not their fault because they still see you every day and when you are trying to offload it gets translated into nothing more dramatic than 'Chris is having a hard time' or 'Chris is having a moan' so the universal inability to interpret the unexpressed means that they do *not* see the signs, and before anybody knows it, you make a big statement that is way beyond their vision and you are all but dead.

It *was* a cry for help, but in the moment, I did not think help was an option. Of course, it was a cry for help. Time

46

helps you understand that. The only Plan B then seemed the exit.

So, I was quite stunned to actually be awake in hospital, lovingly cared for by people who wanted to save me in that selfless NHS way without knowing my circumstance. That kept me alive, for which I am truly grateful, despite my own stupidity. I do not know the names of the nurses or if indeed they now realise it was me, but I owe the world to them, along with my Mum, who called for help. In that split second when the game was up, I was given a chance to fight another day. When I came around, I just cried and cried, balling my eyes out in front of my Nan and sister, who did not really understand why.

Within two days, I was discharged with all kinds of tablets and no kind of help. More pills, but this time with the right approach. I felt that 48 hours after was probably too soon and putting me back together consisted of a package of anti-depressants and medicine that, in time, didn't work because I rejected them. There was no mental health aftercare. I was just let go with medicine.

The fall-out was colossal. I decided to look after my Nan almost full time. But I had developed an anxiety twitch where my arm would just descend into a world of its own. I learnt to control my depression, but my anxiety could be set off at the smallest trigger.

The knock-on effect was that when I applied for jobs, they asked for my medical records and that meant securing work was hard. They would contact my previous employer and then they would have to explain a period of absence due to illness and sickness. I felt, that in every sense, I had to start again. My singing career was adrift, my mind was all at sea and I was oceans apart from regaining the confidence to begin once more.

I was trying to get well and build some stability. That only meant one thing. Health was a priority and the dream was dead.

I did make a vague limp-wristed attempt at a 'comeback', not that I had a career to return from. I was going through the motions. I went into a recording studio to nail down a song that a friend had written for me after my attempt on my life. The song was called *Way In The World,* and I thought it was exceptional enough to send to 50 A & R people in the business, but the truth is that I was not well and it was not.

It was a poor throw of the dice. Those close to me could see I still wanted it. I knew the years were against me. Mentally, I didn't know if I was strong enough and the rejection that came in the shape of no responses whatsoever pretty much slammed the door shut in my face. I needed help – mentally, and I needed a guardian angel professionally.

Thankfully, behind my back somebody waved a magic wand. Oh, and I had bumped into Gary in town, completely by chance. Maybe things were meant to be. Perhaps there was a shining star in the distance.

Chapter Nine

Of course, I had watched the *X Factor* year in year out. I had laughed and cried and wondered how and why. I had questioned the joke acts and sympathised with the ones that, in my eyes, appeared to have been manipulated. I had shouted at the judges and watched the varying fates of the winners. In short, I knew its history, but I was fan. To me, it was the talent show to be on.

My over-riding memory as a viewer was seeing Alexandra Burke performing with Beyoncé in 2008. My heart skipped a beat at that iconic performance. I got lost in the dream that I could be up there with my hero, and I voted time after time for Alexandra on the strength of that performance, continually shouting at the TV 'Keep going, I am voting for you'.

The problem was I couldn't *see* myself there. Every year I had sent off for an application form and each time I had filled it in, but then put it in the drawer and not sent it off. I doubted myself too much. I really thought it was a step too far. Alexandra was a normal person when she entered. I was watching her in the final with one of the world's biggest stars. In an instant, I could not see where she had come from. I only saw the finished act. I did not even remember her at the audition stage. I could only see the end product. It was way too far away, asking to achieve the impossible.

So, I dreamt and wondered. I applied and withdrew. It was too much.

Gary and Nan had seen the yearly adverts inviting people to apply. They knew I had come so close to entering in previous years and they believed, especially Gary of course, that I had something. I could not see the wood for the trees any more. I no longer knew if I had a talent. Bar the promotion on the cruise ship, there were no real highs and plenty of lows, with the nasty side of the business and its loneliness leaving me with little to cling to. The fact that I had returned early from most cruise gigs through whatever circumstances both shook me personally and made me disbelieve. Maybe, I was not cut out for it, perhaps I hadn't seen enough in myself to guts it out. Anxiety and self-doubt meant that I could no longer hear my own voice. Your mental health wavers and, because of that, I no longer felt I had something special.

But then I got the phone call that changed my life...and that lack of confidence and anxiety only escalated.

I was delirious when I put the phone down, grateful for the put-up job, but convinced it had been a wind-up, cusping my hands to my mouth shouting 'Oh my God' on repeat to the heavens in anything from a whisper to a Tarzan-like cry. *They* had called me. Would I come for an audition?

Yes, of course, I would. No, there is no way on the planet. What am I going to sing? What do I wear? How does it work? I don't think I can do this. I have to do this. This is bigger than anything I have ever done. This is too big for me. My mind was playing ping pong with itself. The two halves of my brain were in complete contradiction with each other. Counting down the days to audition sent me into over-drive. Keeping a lid on it at work was near impossible, having to rein it in whilst daydreaming through the long hours of calls. At home, I was a nightmare, biting every nail and not knowing whether to thank or curse Gary and my Nan. Finally, the day came.

It is now April 2012, and I arrive early at the Liverpool Echo Arena. Sometimes great venues make great talent rise to the occasion. I shrink into the spiralling queue, unaware of what lies ahead, amid a sea of faces whose dreams would inevitably be torn apart within the next few hours. I recognise nobody and hardly talk to a soul. Some are buzzing, convinced the world would fall at their feet; others are deep in thought, trying to get some focus. For everybody, there is a long way to go – both in terms of the queue and of course, the show. The final is eight months away.

Dare to dream, they say, but I think you have to do it in stages. And I was not even past the first door into the building yet. The queue is not a good place for the soul when you are waiting for your moment. So much time to kill and a lifetime of flashbacks that got you here to contemplate. I saw it all in my own mental TV montage – from the much-maligned cruise ships to my Granddad's last words to me, all mixed in with clips of *X Factors* past. This was all in my head. Those winners and near-misses all started in a queue like me, yet I believed them all to be stars. And yet, they too had come from waiting in line with nothing but a number on their chest.

In moments of calmness, I told myself that I had nothing to lose, but these respites were few and far between. The reality was that I would have one moment to impress, and if I failed and had the mental strength, then I could have another moment another year, as so many had done before. If it wasn't too late.

Finally, the moment came when a tired dried throat would be put to the test. Until you have stood in that queue and hit your very first note, you really cannot know how the tension of waiting will manifest itself when the times arrives to impress. Now, I realised too that these were the bits you did not see on the TV. And I thought that I knew the show inside out.

Inside the venue there was no razzmatazz, none of the huge branding or any of the familiar names from the show. Instead, I was directed to come forward to a small black booth and sing. Once I had sung, I am handed a golden ticket from the other side. I am through.

I really am through.

I have no idea what happens next, but I am stunned by how simple and disconnected the experience is. I am almost laughing in complete contrast to my nerves earlier in the day. Is that it? Yes, it is. You are through to the next stage. It was that simple, yet heartbreak had already begun for many. I had only sung for, perhaps, a minute. Now, I had to wait another two hours.

Once my disbelief had subsided at how easy and comical the experience had been, my nerves rose again. I took no confidence from my first audition. Instead, it made me more nervous. My friends kept telling me I could do this. It didn't help. They were my friends. They would have said that even if they didn't believe it, but right now they genuinely did sense something that I had lost sight of in my dizziness.

Two hours later, I am called again. This time, there is no booth. I set eyes on my maker. I am now before someone whom I assume to be a producer. I stand there in my combats not one bit looking the part. My knees are knocking with fear – radiating my tension, but a source of comedy to everyone else.

'Are you OK?' he asked.

'No, I am nervous,' I stuttered.

And they made a note. I reflect now that this may have been for the edit as much as my welfare.

I deliver four lines and then a chorus. I pick my banker song, *The Rose. They* pick me. I am through. Twice in one day. I am speechless. I don't know what to say, nor do I have the words. I should take stock and realise that the little that they have asked me to do has done a lot, and that I am actually sailing through. You can't see it, though. You are in the moment. There is no whiff of big time about this. I have merely survived and I live to fight another day. I have never seen the raw footage of that audition.

Nor do you get to savour the moment. In seconds, I am in the hands of researcher, and now it gets serious. I have to fill in more forms beyond my original application, the contents of which I am oblivious to, as I was at the mercy of Gary and my Nan. I should get a sense now of what is to come. The questions address my character – the tone is whether I have any skeletons in my closet? I simply reply no.

Of course, there were a few, but I gained hold of my senses, which up to now, I had been naïve. I am not sure if it was a lightbulb moment or if those flashbacks from the queue came back to haunt me and I thought that I ought to just shut up. So, I gave them nothing.

When I got home, I was knackered. It had been a surreal day. I had done little but achieved a lot. I had possibly sung less than the duration of an entire track, but the nervous tension of the wait had killed me.

There was a long way to go. I had to wait the best part of a month before the process would resume. One date was circled on my calendar: 23 May 2012. I was at the Liverpool Echo Arena for 0530 in heavy rain. I was told to get there early. Within reason, too. There were thousands there. My family couldn't join me until 0930. That meant four hours getting soaked through.

At the time, I believed this to be normal. I believed them that they wanted ordinary people to just turn up. Get there early to avoid disappointment. They sold you the belief that nobodies could become somebodies. They had the power to make you a star.

Furthermore, Series Eight had been littered with negativity. Judges Tulisa and Louis Walsh had accused contestant Misha B of bullying backstage and mean comments. Gary Barlow had said this stigma had effectively ended her chances in the competition. One entrant, Frankie Cocozza, had also sworn during a live show and had been accused of taking cocaine.

What I have since learned is that the band Union J had been on tour with Westlife, Rylan Clark had starred on a Katie Price modelling show, Ella Henderson had previously filmed for *Come Dine With Me*, Carolynne Poole had been on *Fame Academy* on the BBC and had previously entered *X Factor,* Jahméne had been spotted on *YouTube* and James Arthur had been invited.

I am proud to say that I was a just an ordinary applicant. As I stood there in the queue, even at my age and with the knowledge of the show, I did not yet know any of these people and believed everything to be real.

Every aspect of the programme now kicked up a notch. The branding was everywhere, and runners and cameras were up and down, getting anything and everything – or so it seemed. To this day, I have no idea how they make sense of it all – the edit suite must be littered with thousands of hours of

53

unseen footage. Yet, whilst it all looks so random, it is only with hindsight that now makes me realise otherwise. When you are new to this, you think there are cameras all around, filming non-stop. If I had been able to take step back, I would have seen that, whilst there is an element of that, they came looking for others too.

So, when they started filming my family with me in the queue at 10 am, I thought I had just got lucky. *But* they couldn't film everyone. The red light was on me. I couldn't have been a more unprepared pop star, waiting for my turn and getting by on cheese and piccalilli sandwiches, stuffing my face with heartburn-inducing crisps and cokes. This was standard fare for a Maloney picnic – the boredom and the nerves forcing me to pile it on.

And there was too much time to think. I was terrified – my nervous system rejecting me again. On the TV, it looks like a party atmosphere in the queue. I do not recall it as that. There was no collective fun. Instead, I compared myself to everyone, making judgements on if they looked the part and talking myself out of it, and that was before I heard some of the amazing voices warming up or playing to the cameras. In a nutshell, I felt way out of my depth.

The queue moved at a snail's pace. It was a long time before we even got inside the arena and then, like a ride at Disney where you turn a corner expecting that you will be on in a minute, you groan as, before you, another line snakes its way around a bend, beyond which you cannot see. Then, around that corner, you are moved to a first holding area, followed by a second one, and before you know it, it is getting dark outside.

It is very difficult to explain and control the three mood swings you experience in the queue – utter fear and no belief, moments of calm and reflection and then the horrific moment when you are actually one act short of the stage. The gear change in your adrenaline levels is matched in your heart rate, your sweat, and the hollowness in your stomach. If my knees were knocking last time, now my whole bowel department was

54

about to give way. The stupid thing is you know it is coming and it is all you have ever wanted to do. I had dreamt about standing on that X on the stage in my hometown and now it was here such a positive mental image was the one that was destroying me.

Ten minutes before, I am told that I am singing *Hello* by Lionel Richie. I do not understand why they are doing this. I feel like there is manipulation at play.

I can't go on. I am absolutely terrified. The camera is pointing in my face and Dermot O' Leary is trotting out lines he has uttered a thousand times before, radiating calm and exuding compassion in that Dermot way.

Suddenly the tension gets worse. The act on before me are getting booed off. I panic at their rejection. I don't know if it is the noise of the lion's den that distresses me or the public humiliation and lack of love. They now have to walk past me. All I can hear is what sounds like a pack of wolves. The real sound of what is going on around me is lost. I no longer hear Dermot. I can't make out the runner calling my name. Slow-mo kicks in, coupled with fast-forward. I am rooted to the spot, legs like jelly, unable to move, but at the same time seemingly hurtling towards that cauldron out there.

It is the biggest job interview of my life, yet if there were a trap door, I would take it. There is no way I can walk out onto…

And then I suddenly on-stage, feeling as though I have been pushed on. A researcher or a runner leaves me no choice, their hand thrusting me into a glaring spotlight, and towards a table with four of the most famous faces on television in front of me. Gary Barlow, Geri Halliwell, Tulisa and Louis Walsh. Two of these are my idols. I have seen this scenario on TV so many times. I have tried to envisage me here plenty more. If I was a scared bunny beforehand, I am now a rabbit in the headlights.

I freeze. I can't find the X on the stage. The mob will soon be shouting, I am sure. I can not utter a word. The silence is as destructive as the deafening noise before. You can hear a pin drop.

Geri Halliwell suddenly rises from her seat and is walking towards me. Now, I am even more terrified. None of this is choreographed. I am glued to the spot.

'Deep breaths…you can do it,' she whispers, barely picked up by a microphone.

'We are ready when you are.'

I shake some more. It is now or never. My quivering turns into something resembling a nod and I move towards the X. I feel as though I have been under pressure for God knows how many hours and the result is that my confidence is at an all-time low. Now the reality of my dream scenario has hit me too. I have never been on a stage to 10,000 people and this is the venue I wanted to do it at. I am treading the boards at the Echo Arena. If I can't hold it together, then this will be my one and only performance here. My jaw feels locked.

The music starts and for a second, I am in delay. Then it starts to carry me along and its rhythm takes me from one trance like state to another.

I can feel the intro swelling. I know my cue inside out. My dry throat has to deliver. I am almost waiting on myself to check that sound emerges from it.

And then, the next thing I hear is applause and all I have sung is the opening line.

'Some say love…'

The place erupts. But I hardly hear them. I can see them, but my vocal and the backing track have finally become my only distraction. All the other soundtracks have now gone. I have caught up with the moment and am thriving in it. Was it my best vocal ever? I don't know. Was it one of those Susan Boyle moments where the image presented to them on stage afforded no realistic expectation, and therefore doubled its appreciation value when I actually showed that I could sing? Possibly. Was it because it was my home crowd too? I certainly would rather not have been anywhere else.

I complete the whole song. I am not booed off. But Gary Barlow is shaking his head. I will be devastated if I have not shown my hero what I can do.

My knees begin to tremble again. Tears are rolling down my cheeks. It is done and it is over. No more. I cannot put myself through this ever again. My emotions are spilling over at relief and nothing more. For a second that consumes me and I almost forget that they have voted on me. Then, in delay, I see the audience standing. I try to see a familiar face, but there are none – just a cacophony of noise, but without exception, in support.

Then the arena calms. I feel fantastic now, but still an exhausted nervous wreck.

Silence.

They ask me about the song choice. I have switched it back to *The Rose*. I explain to them that I had played it at my Granddad's funeral. They ask where Nan is but they know she is waiting in the wings. They call her on and the place explodes.

Nan revels in the reaction it, but it tips me over the edge. Looking back, it was the most beautiful moment with the perfect person. I couldn't have been more emotional at the time and yet now, happier to reflect on it. I realise too that I have given them perfect television.

'How the hell have you kept that voice quiet?' Gary smiles.

'I have never put myself out there.' I have no idea what to say, but I reply in broad tearful Scouse.

I am at my most innocent, and it shows in that phrase, which in the months ahead would be turned around to paint me as a liar. I *had* put myself out there by working the cruise ships, they would argue. Of course, it is true. But I had never put myself out *there*.

'Don't come on here,' I explained I had been warned against it. 'You are gonna embarrass yourself.'

'Who said that?' one of the four replied.

I could barely see them in the light.

'People,' was all I could offer in response, with a downbeat tone of resignation.

'Let's take a vote,' Gary reined them all in.

I am now returning to the out of body experience. The audience have been magnificent. Yet, somehow it is back to square one, and it may mean nothing. I am so nervous that I genuinely have convinced myself that it can only go one way.

Then, they set me free – from the moment and years of self-doubt.

They put me through.

The noise is deafening again as I leave the stage, unsure where to go and oblivious to how I am coming across. I have no words, just painful facial expressions as a lifetime of angst dissipates itself in that moment.

The crew are still rolling and there is Dermot by the stage.

'Well done, Maloney,' he offers as though we are old school mates, but in that Dermot way where he has always been friends with everyone.

'You're through to bootcamp,' he bellows.

But I do not hear him, as though that is not really the prize. My 'success' is that I conquered my nerves and delivered.

'Oh yeah, I am,' I reply a moment after, slowly catching up.

I am in dreamland. The next stage is so far away in reality that there is no stage. This is my moment and I feel as though I have won it. I have done enough and my ambitions are fulfilled.

There are cameras everywhere. I am now whisked off to see Olly Murs and Caroline Flack for the *Xtra Factor*.

It is now approaching 1 am. Nan is OK, but it is way past my bedtime. I had been aware of other contestants getting camera time, but now they are all pointing our way. Everybody else has gone home. I begin to say the words, 'I am through to bootcamp' over and over again. My head is spinning as I hit the sack.

I remember almost nothing of the previous 24 hours except the very last bit, standing before my idols and faces that I know through the TV, and doing so in front of my home crowd, banishing demons in the process.

I do not sleep a wink. It is like a bad dream in its cluttered disorganisation in my head. But I stay awake and, of course, it is all good. It is fantastic.

The next morning reality hits. I have to go back to work.

Chapter Ten

Some of my work colleagues had been in the audience. For the rest, we couldn't say a word. I suppose they all began to find out, but it was never mentioned, and I had to sit down with bosses and explain what might be happening. Again.

I think the next day I was floating so much that I probably had my best day ever at the call centre. I was trying to begin that process of taking each day as it comes, because I had been let down before I found myself daring to believe a little. It remained a daydream, though.

I was riding that wave so much that I had not processed any of it, and when I began to settle, I realised that I had to get my act together. I was no pop star – my clothes were shocking. I needed to think about the whole thing and raise my game before bootcamp, where many younger people with less inhibition and much more natural instinct for television would essentially start becoming my rivals, even if they were not going to be in my category. It was time to lose the t-shirt and cardigan.

Then I started to worry about song choices. Was I getting ahead of myself or preparing appropriately? I realise now that I was always going to look for the next thing to stress over, even though, as the days passed, I could for the first time in ages feel some self-belief rising. I settled on *Million Love Songs* by Take That. Gary Barlow had written it and that could go either way for me, but I felt he had been warm to me so, tactically, I thought it was astute. I was slowly developing an edge and a sense of what lay ahead, but it had taken me an eternity to think like this.

A never-ending week passed before I heard anything, but then received an email to tell me that bootcamp would be over a long weekend in a fortnight's time – and best of all, it would be in Liverpool. That put to bed immediately all those bad memories of saying goodbye and boarding cruise ships. I was safe for the duration.

Then they told me that I would have to live at home and come in every day, which I thought placed me at a disadvantage, so I objected. I needed to get in the same zone as the others and stay there, even though there would be no respite from the pressure. I could see on this occasion that to be removed from the stress of it all would mean I was so detached from the process and that I could really lose pace with the others.

It was the right decision. I knew too that if I got no further, I did not have to travel half the country heartbroken to get home. I would just get on the bus and head to Nan's and it would all be over, and soon I would be back in my comfort zone. Equally, if I needed anything – and I had heard a few horror stories about bootcamps – I could just ring Mum and she would bring it in.

Of course, the night before, my anxiety returned. I had worked all week and begun to talk myself into a position where I was not going to go, despite my earlier clarity. Somehow, I got myself there, rooming with Kye Sones and two others, befriending mostly the Liverpudlians, but generally keeping myself to myself.

But you had to mix because, as you will have seen on the shows over the years, one of the ways that they whittle down the boot-campers is by having them share a song. So, whatever impact you made at your audition, was now watered down by the fact that you were in effect part of a group.

Some acts are born to be stars, others are best playing second fiddle. There is often one who wants to take over and for us that was Colin Malcolm. We looked awful too. I was in a hoodie and jeans, and perhaps the Overs (older age) category weren't meant to be style icons, especially at this stage, but we really didn't look the part. Add to that – our dance moves were predictably appalling.

To make matters worse, the song we were singing was one I would never choose. Yes – they were taking me out of my comfort zone from my audition, but beyond that, I hadn't been given the tools yet to shine.

And we only had half an hour to learn it. So, it came as no surprise that we fucked it up. When they put Kye through, I decided in my head that it was all pre-determined. I was starting to catch up with how the show worked, even though as a viewer I had got it instantly. Living it in real time was an altogether different situation.

But then they put me through. I had already mentally got on the bus home. The audition was so bad that I don't think they even showed it. Somehow, I survived. When you see others progress, and you think it is in the script, you don't ever consider the same of yourself. There was no way I should still be in the competition after murdering the *Kings of Leon,* but somehow, I was.

My self-belief was swinging like a pendulum. I had messed it up, but they liked it. I had written myself off, but got a reprieve. I think, especially in the Overs, some of the younger contestants could smell the fear on us. That last chance saloon syndrome met the carefreeness of youth halfway. We knew it was now or never, and I only realised how we were perceived when one of them stopped me and left a real stain of negativity and paranoia on me.

'You really, really want this, don't you?' she quizzed.

I didn't know who she was, but this person got to me with such a simple question.

'Don't you want it?' She re-phrased the question.

Then walked away, looking at me.

It rattled me. I questioned everything and could never properly evaluate how I was coming across. Was it that obvious?

Of course, by the time I walked out the next day on to the stage of the Liverpool Echo in front of 10,000 of my own crowd, my nerves were the first topic of conversation.

'This is the last chance I have got to turn my nerves into something positive,' I told Gary Barlow, and then launched into his song, *A Million Love Songs.*

I know from watching the show back that either Tulisa or Nicole said I had stepped up, while Gary, who seemed to be championing me, had no issues with my song choice. You can hear him say, 'What a voice' amidst the noise of the arena. Yet, the judges were saying Kye had become the one to watch now.

I got a great reaction, but I knew that it was not as good as my first audition. That could be down to a number of reasons – the lateness in the day and my Nan coming on, or maybe I just wasn't as good, and nor was my song choice this time around.

It *felt* good and that counted for a lot, because if I could banish some anxiety in the midst of all this then that would really help me in the long term. But I did get a great reception, and I think being in Liverpool gave me that confidence. I felt the crowd wanted me to do well, and I felt that I had done the song justice in front of one of my idols.

We had to wait until the Sunday afternoon, when they would announce who would be whittled down from what must have been 200 remaining acts. It was an exhaustive process and, by the end of the weekend, people were keeping themselves to themselves and I can say that, with the exception of Rylan, I actually hadn't got to know a soul.

Rylan, who is probably known to you now through his TV work since, couldn't help but draw attention to himself, made him stand out as bags of fun!

Finally, the moment of truth came and they lined us up in fives on the stage as though we were about to be shot. You forget that the cameras are there. They are everywhere, but when you are staring at the judges there are only two things on your mind – I am going home, I am staying. On repeat. I have never felt particularly lucky and I didn't now. You really do expect someone else to get the nod.

Then they called a tea break and the tension just escalated. I was making no sense at all, unable to keep still, eyes still popping out. The rabbits were back in the headlights. The longer it went on, the more I was going home, but of course, that makes no sense at all. We were just the next in line. And it was one hell of a queue.

They call us back and I am now looking for anything that will help me. I begin saying a prayer and making the sign of a cross. I have seen some of the acts who had already departed and am genuinely shocked. She is still in. I know this is potentially a blood bath.

'Please call my name out,' I whisper to myself. 'Please let it be me.'

You watch this stuff year after year, and it can look pathetic, but when you are standing there with a racing heart and you know it is the last chance, this is how you feel.

And they call my name. I cannot believe it.

'Fuck, fuck, fuck,' is all I was thinking. 'Thank God,' quickly follows.

I am relieved but scared some more.

The truth is that my stress levels were probably going to come in about the same if I had got through or hadn't. It was that much of a high and equivalent low, but it produced the same set of chemical reactions within me to the degree that I instantly did not want to go to something that I had wanted so much. This had been the most intense environment I had ever known, but logic should have told me that it would only get worse from here. I did not really understand why I was putting myself through this. I sensed an attack on my nervous system coming. If I could only step back and see that the odds had never been more in my favour. I had already seen off so many people whom I hadn't seen at all. Thousands were gone. A handful remained. The pressure was going up – yes, but the deal was better.

Chapter Eleven

I had left around five in the evening, slipping out the back way thinking that was a smart idea, when of course fans were long since wise to this. I was crying my eyes out, panicking at what was next and emotional that I finally had arrived at this point. Inactivity through suspense equals exhaustion – that was the lesson of the weekend. I just wanted to get home, but I couldn't even get a cab so, classic Scouse, I went to the chippy and faced my new reality. I had work in the morning.

I felt a fraud. Of course, I was told not to say anything back in the office. Apart from those who had seen my first audition, nobody really knew that I could sing. I tuned out of much of the work conversation because all I was thinking was that I wanted Gary as my judge. He had been the nicest and most encouraging, but I also loved and respected his work.

It was soon confirmed. There would now be two Garys in my life.

I just lied at work. I told them that I hadn't got through. I really did want to announce it to the world, but it wasn't worth it. It was a façade though because they could all see me going in to tell the bosses and performing this ridiculous scenario where I turned all the chairs round so management's backs were facing out to the staff!

Then, I began talking like a ventriloquist, only half opening my mouth but telling my bosses to look sad and not to react. Eventually, I told them.

'I will need some time off work.' I got practical.

'I am really sorry to hear that,' they played along. 'Now, go back and start work!'

You can probably imagine that every day I waited for news of what was next. I knew it was Judges' Houses but I had no idea where or when. I just prayed for one thing. I did not want to be swanning off to somewhere like Miami and have to fly back with everyone else if they had kicked me out. The same mindset I had for the Liverpool auditions. I had never really thought about that aspect of the *competition* until recently. I noticed too that at this stage I started to use that word rather than thinking it was a TV show. It was fast becoming a contest.

I waited and waited and first there was nothing. Then there was a date and it got moved. I knew that the other categories had already gone and we were left waiting. On 4 August 2012 tragedy had struck. Gary Barlow's wife Dawn had given birth to Poppy Barlow. Terribly, Poppy didn't make it. She was stillborn. Understandably, we had to wait.

By the time it came to film, Gary wanted to be as close to home as possible, so for all those years when you have seen glorious sunsets and beautiful beaches at the judges' houses, we got Northampton!

We de-camped to the incredible 11,000 acres of Boughton House, just near Kettering – a French style stately home with more art and porcelain than you will ever see in your entire lifetime.

Six of us now had to become three. Brad, Melanie, Nicola, Carolynne, Kye and myself were all fighting it out to appear on the live shows. Friendships were left at the door…

I did not rate my chances. Melanie and Kye had great voices, Carolynne had been on before. Your mind, you see, started to calculate.

I began to relax a little, getting to know Dermot a bit and many of the runners on the show who were really lovely, but I didn't really get on well with Caroline Flack working the *Xtra Factor* show on ITV2. Cheryl Cole was back as Gary's assistant, but I didn't feel like I hit it off with her.

I started to become much more aware in real time of how they were making the show. When you are in a queue for hours with thousands of other people, you play up to the camera, but it is fleeting stardom. Now, because there were so few of us, you really could see the cogs turning, even though you wouldn't fully understand why until you got home and the series aired.

When I came to watch it with everyone else, it just looked like I was in tears all the time.

I trotted out all the clichés, but I meant them sincerely.

'I want to do myself proud. I want to make my family proud,' I declared.

And by the time I was due to go in front of Gary and Cheryl, my anxiety was rising again, despite having been relatively tranquil since arrival.

I walked through the pansies in the garden and there they were, the two of them, sat in front of me, in what would look the most relaxed setting in the world. Instead, it was riddled with tension. To the side – three violinists and one pianist, whom I had barely met before. Ahead – Gary and Cheryl.

'Hello.' I took a sharp intake of breath and mouthed to him as though I had walked in on two naked people in front of me.

'Every time I see you, you are nervous,' Gary began. 'What's the deal with the nerves?'

I looked like my world was going to collapse when I watch it back.

'You're just fantastic,' I replied pathetically and adoringly. 'You're just brilliant.'

I was auditioning in front of my hero again and coming across like a fan.

'You've got to stop that,' he interrupted. 'From thousands of people, you're here in the last six. This is a fantastic moment. You should celebrate today. This is a fantastic moment in your life. What's there to worry about?'

He spoke the truth – but I can only see it today.

My mind was on the first line of Air Supply's *'All Out of Love'.*

When I finished, I looked sheepish, but I felt I had done OK, despite the fact that some of the strings were out of time.

'Christopher, thank you so much,' was all Gary said.

And I walked off.

Dermot was not so much waiting for me as ready to pounce, and I informed him that I thought it went well. While I was telling him it was the biggest audition of my life and I had sung my heart out, Cheryl was telling Gary that I had a big voice and the public would love me.

Gary was concerned that I was too frightened and he couldn't get me on a stage on a Saturday night. Cheryl said it was going to be the best Overs ever, but, as sincere as she might have been, I feel now that this was part of the narrative. In my view, there was a real sense on the show that it had fallen short of its promise, in that it had not delivered a success story in the Overs category. Gary said he wanted to sleep on it.

I didn't feel I could do any more. It was out of my hands now. Next, I had to walk into this ostentatious room, with its paintings and raging fire to face the others on camera. I had been last to go, and Brad was first to greet me on my return – except I only half acknowledged him and went straight to hug Kye and then the girls. Now, I had to wait. Saturday night in the middle of Northamptonshire with just time to kill. It was getting dark by 7 pm and there was nothing to do except raid the mobile canteen and walk back on my own, alone with my thoughts.

It was then that I went for the walk and saw the shooting star.

I took it as a sign and made a wish that I got through. I had never seen one before, and it seemed to be the final piece in the jigsaw. I *was* meant to be here singing for Granddad, to one of my heroes. Finally, I belonged. The stars really were coming out for me tonight.

But it was the next day that counted. In the morning, I packed, fearing that I was heading home, had breakfast and then had to do more filming. It was a gruelling schedule.

Of course, I hadn't slept so that just over-egged the tears, and I worked myself into a state, saying how embarrassed I would be to go home, having not got through. I was sobbing again.

I was the penultimate to be called – unaware of the fate of the others. Melanie was left waiting.

'I felt you had a great day yesterday,' Gary began. 'I don't need to remind you of the amazing reaction you have had at every audition.'

My eyes were now so red, waterworks at full throttle.

'That first audition…everyone was crying. People spend years trying to mastermind that and you just seem to have it.'

It was starting to look as though the star was shining brightly for me. Then he changed tack and it dimmed.

'Your nerves scare the living daylight out of me. Those emotions are hard to conquer.'

'I will do the work,' I interrupted him, nodding and sobbing.

'It's not the work,' he replied calmly. 'This has been my hardest decision. I am dealing with people's lives here.'

And he crushed me.

'You are not in my final three.'

Chapter Twelve

'OK, that's great, it's been great,' I replied without knowing the words that came out of my mouth.

I just found myself gibbering out my gratitude. But somehow, I did mean it too. The stress had been enormous and that was now over. I was sad but also glad. The shooting star had passed and didn't have my name on it.

I walked away, It was time to go home.

I didn't see the three who had got through. The show now goes into lockdown. It was the end of the road, but also an outpouring of nervous tension. The dream was dead. So near and yet so far.

I was surprised how well I was coping. As much as I wanted it, maybe it was not as much as I thought. I just thought I had given it my all and it was not meant to be, but I had done bloody well to get this far. I sat there for a couple of hours weighing it all up, not so much with steam dripping off me, but emotions seeping through me.

I didn't need to go home embarrassed.

I had begun to process what had happened and think about the train back and what lay ahead. Back to the call centre tomorrow morning, answering phones, rather than have people pick them up to vote for me. It didn't matter. I had achieved something very few others had managed.

Then, from nowhere, my star flickered back into orbit.

'Chris, I need to talk to you,' a producer confided.

I was somewhat taken aback. Not more filming, please.

'Gary wants to see you,' she said.

I thought I would never see him again.

I was escorted away.

When we got to Gary, I should have twigged that something was up. The cameras were rolling again – and I was all set to leave.

'Chris,' he began calmly, but with dramatic flair, 'I have been told by the producers that I can take one more to the live shows.'

'Really?' I began to tremble again.

I started to think it is back on again. I began to believe.

'It's down to the public,' he explained. 'They have got to vote.'

I can do this. I can do this. I realise that my words of consolation and relief had been premature. Yes – I was relieved that the stress was over, but of course, I still wanted it. What had I been thinking?

I hadn't wanted to give any more of me. That was the point. I was fine. I wanted to go home. Now I was back, and I would do anything. That mood swing was both a reflection on me and the emotional strings that the show can pull.

I had briefly stepped out of the process for a couple of hours, and resigned to my fate. Now, I am back at the railway station saying goodbye to some of the others, whom I had been kept apart from, and contemplating the journey home with a completely different attitude, knowing that I couldn't tell anyone once again. That is a very difficult thing to accomplish when you are on a train for three hours.

By the time I got home, they were all waiting for me. The script could have been so different:

'Right sit down,' I was now doing the Gary Barlow on my family.

'Are you through or what? Dad asked.

'I am through, but I am not.' That was the only honest way I could put it.

Dad became more frustrated than me, beginning to lose his temper.

'I didn't get through to the live shows, but I am through,' I tried to explain.

They didn't really understand.

The truth was I didn't really understand either.

Chapter Thirteen

'Hello, love?' Rylan Clark was the first to greet me. 'How you doing, darling?'

What have I got myself into, I wondered? I knew instantly that I did not fit in. Bootcamp was up a notch from auditions and Judges' Houses topped that, but now we were dealing with some proper talent. I thought *3 Red,* together with Amy Mottram had amazing voices, while Adam Burgess had an edge. Then there was *Union J*, Ella Henderson and James Arthur. It was a tough field, and already on day one at the signing of contracts I felt the heat rise. I was left alone in a corner, and felt that the others did not respect me because I had got through via what they may have perceived as a back door. Without knowing if it were a TV gimmick or whether I had genuinely come 'fourth' out of six in Northamptonshire, I wondered whether they felt that I had not earned a place.

They were taking extra care this year too. There had been problems in the previous series in the contestants' house with the Frankie Cocozza stuff, but this year there was no house, so we all de-camped to the top floor of the Corinthia Hotel, which I felt was detrimental to mood and independence. When I would have prepared meals for myself, I began to live off a diet of hake and new potatoes, making McDonald's the only alternative.

By the time we meet in London, the show begins to air almost straightaway. I am re-living it in real time too as you do, watching the final cut of my own audition, and am quietly pleased with how I sung. How I come across is another issue. My phone goes into meltdown. Work goes crazy. And I can't walk into shops in Liverpool without people being genuinely kind. Everywhere I go cars are beeping their horns. I don't know if this happens in every city or that it is just Liverpool, but it explodes overnight. This is my first taste of fame and I am bewildered at the reaction.

It was so different from the times I used to get off a stop early on the bus to avoid being beaten up, or snuck back into town for drama nights with my Dad berating me for not having eyes on a proper job, and perhaps the most revealing 'moment' in the screening of the auditions was his reaction.

'You kept that a bit quiet,' he said reminiscent of what Gary had said to me at audition.

But now it was game on, in the knowledge that by the next Sunday, I could still be going home again, and my brush with fame would have lasted no more than fifteen minutes.

I was caught in a whirlwind, my feet scarcely touching the ground. I spent the least amount of my time singing. It was constant media, with interview after interview, and I had no training or experience in this area. I kept my counsel small and if they asked a question where I feared dirty tricks, I just ducked it. They wanted you to come unstuck, your vulnerability was a currency for newspaper print. We only made it into the studio on the first Thursday. The *X Factor* juggernaut had well and truly rolled into town.

As that first week flew by, I just felt I was constantly behind in the ballgame, and felt pretty uncomfortable around the Overs in particular – wildcard positioned me as an unjustified threat, and I felt like that transferred itself to me personally. I knew I was I out of my depth.

Others were taking part in a TV show. For Rylan, it was the whole package. Welcome to showbiz. Fair play to him – he made his assault on the business. *I* just wanted to conquer my nerves and prove I could sing. That is daft because I had already done that of course on numerous ships.

Gary Barlow was very much hands-on. He did, after all, have a major track record both in the studio and live that the other three judges could not match. As an individual, I got the sense that if he couldn't do something full-on, he wouldn't do it at all and would expect the same from you. I did not personally see that in the others. I felt I was definitely with the right mentor.

But even then, with Gary available for three days that week, studio time was at a premium, because the other cogs churned into action, and that meant costume, hair, make up, scenery, props and stage positions. Your average song on the show would last a maximum of three minutes. The duration of the show was invariably three times longer than all of the singing put together. That, in a nutshell, is the machine.

By the time Saturday came, I was already feeling burnt out. It was just constant, flitting from one requirement to another at the request of the programme, and at the expense of honing your act. I only had to sing for those handful of minutes, but really felt I hadn't put any work into that bit at all. I had sought solace by retreating to the basement of the hotel to practise my vocal alone, benefitting from the good acoustics at the foot of the building. Downtime was priceless.

On the Saturday, I am at Fountain Studios for 0830. The live show is nearly twelve hours away. My appearance will very likely be fleeting.

But I *am* excited too.

Most of my family, including my Mum, Gary, my Nan and my sister came down for what could be my one and only performance. The bills were racking up, making it to the final might have bankrupt us! Return trains and a deal at the Europe Hotel for two to three nights a week meant that Mum had to take out a loan just to be there.

They came to see my dream become a reality, and initially that meant meeting superficial aspirations. I had ticked off being in a live TV studio for the first time. Then I wanted to stand on that X again. I needed to get focussed though, because it could all be over in an instant. I had a one in four chance against Amy Mottram, Times Red, and Adam Burridge. Standing on that stage and on that X reminded me why I was here. I did want it badly and I did not want to let anyone down.

It is now 6 October 2012. One hour before we go live and I cannot eat. I am seeking re-assurance from everybody. The opening show is called 'Heroes Night' for some reason. A few London 2012 Olympians are in the audience. One Direction make a brief appearance.

We are live and our appearance is short. At the top of the show Dermot O'Leary announces, 'Let's bring on the wildcards' and I continue to shake. Dermot tries to make light: 'This shaking thing is very much your default position.'

But I was petrified, and seemingly more so than anyone else, and more so than on other occasions.

When he did, I started crying again.

'Well done, buddy, you gotta hold it together,' he patted me on the back with comforting words.

He was a live presenter with years of experience, and somebody was talking in his ear telling him to move to the next junction in the show. I was a nobody, frozen in the moment, with millions of people watching, and no real clue how any of this worked. The release of tension took over, my fists punching the sky. I had made it through to the live shows, even though I was on the live show and this could still be…my last live show.

That, in a sentence, sums up, the fine margins and the high emotions, because I then had about fifteen minutes to change and get back out there and sing for survival again. You survived to become the wildcard, but then you have to fight again to stay in the competition. There was no time to take it in. If anything, I got worse, failing to see that the force of momentum was with me and that my Liverpool audition clips had resonated either through my voice or my character.

Instead, I was shitting it. At the back of your mind, you start to think of your 'Save Me' song, which you may be called upon for if you are in the bottom two the following night. So, your mind is already distracted with that, even though it is the next day's pressure. The reality is that without having taken in the huge vote of confidence that I later discovered was almost two thirds of the public vote to stay in the competition, I was absolutely terrified that I did not know the words. I had been given Mariah Carey's *Hero* to sing to start my competition proper.

I did not have a chance to speak to the other wildcards once I was announced, so can only imagine what their reactions were.

District 3 open the actual show. James Arthur is next, followed by Melanie Masson, Lucy Spraggan and MK1. Then it is me – sixth on.

They run my tape. It is all about the nerves. I hug Gary Barlow about 50 times. They play on my Granddad. I am shocked when I walk out to sing for the first time. It is one thing in plain clothes at a walk through for the show…it is another when Dermot just calls the wildcard winner. Now, I am dazzled by the lights, and have to hit vocals and work camera angles, whilst dealing with a song, which is, as always, an edit of the hit people know.

'I'm so worried about the nerves.' Gary Barlow's comments echo as the package concludes.

In three minutes, it is over. I am relieved and think I have done well enough. I cannot legislate for the public. Have they used their money to vote for me once and my luck is up or are they backing me again, having sent me through the first time? Then there are the judges' comments to negotiate:

'Who was that up there? I don't even recognise you,' Nicole began.

She begins to describe me as a burger with cheese. It feels like a scripted line, and the first of many visits from her to the delicatessen.

'The public have voted you in, so they obviously like you.' It seemed that Louis Walsh was not so sure. 'You have a new colour,' he continued. 'Have you been on a cruise ship recently?'

The two seeds were planted. Nicole offered cheese. Louis re-visited the standard show put down – that I was only fit to sing in the middle of the ocean to a bunch of pensioners.

Tulisa criticised me and never really deviated from that position for the majority of the time. Gary made light telling me, 'no more sunbeds'.

He was backing me though. The studio audience were mostly positive. All that mattered were the phones. Union J, Jade Ellis, Rylan, Kye, Ella Henderson, Carolynne Poole and Jahmene Douglas were still to go. I was pretty much in the middle of the pack. Ella belts out *Rule The World.* To me, it seemed that Lucy Spraggan did not really want to be there. She wrote and performed her own material, and her audition song, *Last Night* had gone straight into the charts. Ella ultimately went on to support Take That three years later.

There was the group song, *Read All About It,* originally performed by Emily Sandé. I had barely been part of any of the rehearsals for it because I had been so late to the final line up. The result was that I barely got a line and ended up at the back of the stage.

By Sunday night, the votes were closed, and my gut feeling was that Carolynne was not staying. The decision went to deadlock with both her and Rylan sharing two votes each. Louis took two minutes to make a decision. Carolynne had less votes than Rylan and had to go. Gary walked off stage in disgust.

It appeared to me that she was fuming, despite what she said to Dermot on camera. Louis had told her to audition again and now she was going home when 24 hours previously I wasn't even in the competition. I felt that she resented me. She then undertook her round of TV commitments that following Monday.

For me, I had survived and I realised then that I was not doing this just for my family or myself. It dawned on me that the public had spent money on me and that I had a responsibility to them to do my best in return. It took being nowhere near the bottom two to take a step back and think 'Hang on a minute, they had the chance to get rid of you twice, but instead have put you through on both occasions.'

There was a long way to go though, and Gary knew it.

'I'll see you at work Monday morning,' he signed off.

Chapter Fourteen

And that is how he saw it. He would drop off his kids in the morning and turn up without fail the day after the second live show of the weekend. He knew what it took. He had experienced good and bad times himself, and witnessed the demons of others around him. Gary had put his name on it and radiated the ultimate professional.

And that incorporated everything from the songs to the advice.

But I was learning. When I watched back my performance, I was stunned to hear that the track on the video playback sounded nothing like it had in the studio on the night. In 2010, it had emerged that the show had been auto-tuning the acts (vocal enhancement), but I had forgotten about all that or assumed it was a scandal that had been put to bed. Now, I was wondering whether it might still be the case, or I was getting used to how different it just sounded in the studio.

Of course, I felt I had the best chance of representing myself in the best light with Gary at the helm, and every week the ritual would begin of him putting a few 80s CDs on, looking for an appropriate song choice, and then he would tinker with an arrangement on the piano in the dance studio to see if it would work for me. Often the appointed vocal coaches or representatives from the record company, Sony, would be there, making their own suggestions. Generally, I agreed with his choices, but I remained very nervous around him.

Once the song was agreed, we would go through a shorter version of exactly how we had picked it for the cameras. After that, the vocal coach would take over. You finished when you finished and cars would pick you up to take you back to the hotel any time between 5 and 9 pm.

The next day, the show would take over. Of course, it's all about the show. People know that over the years very few acts from all those who have entered have gone onto great things but everyone hopes they might be one of the lucky ones. Tuesday was interviews and filming.

It would normally only be by Wednesday that you would work with the choreographer, Brian Friedman, a talented and flamboyant man who made his name working with Britney Spears. Now he was charged with a pair of flat feet from Liverpool. Thursday would invariably mean more press and online chats with question and answers, and then suddenly it was Friday, and the week had evaporated into a pattern of stress, with both non-stop activity and periods of idleness. That relief and exhilaration that you felt on Monday morning soon had swelled into tension by the end of the week when show time loomed, and the long day at Fountain Studios began at the crack of dawn.

Come Friday, the pace was upped a notch. You weren't just trying on clothes or having hair and eye lashes fitted to see what might work. It was now for real. You got a small amount of time on stage walking it through, but it was mostly for the benefit of the cameras trying to put together footage of your judge, casually-dressed and almost 'off camera', to play out on the next day's show. Only one act could obviously appear on the main stage at a time in rehearsal and that hanging around and killing time only served to increase the fears. By the time the cameras rolled on a little one to one between Gary and myself, the theme and tone had been set:

'Christopher, you need to relax' was the soundbite they had begun to repeat regularly.

In the hotel, I was very much alone, and isolated. Personally, I found James hard to talk to and Jahmene not very approachable. Most of the acts had nothing in common with me, nor me with them, but the last through the door status just seemed to exacerbate things.

What I was unable to evaluate in my own head was whether the wildcard status remained good for Week Two. Yes, I reasoned that having voted me *in* the previous week they would have been daft to vote me out at the first hurdle. I also believed that the key demographic of the show was 30

82

plus women and that, therefore, young girls with no credit on their phone would struggle to vote. I clung to the belief too that this show had every type of winner over the years, but perhaps needed an Overs to win it once. The signs were good. I just didn't know it at the time.

The next day I would sing *Alone* – an 80s power ballad from Heart. For some reason it was Love and Heartbreak Week. Former contestant, Rebecca Ferguson, and Taylor Swift were the guest acts. I was grateful for the opportunity to meet a fellow Scouser, who had been there and done it. She knew exactly where my head was and told me to rise above the gimmicks and the put downs, and keep my spirits up. I took great heart from her words. I just needed to remember them when the going got tough.

I was second on the show, following Jahmene. Union J, Ella, James and Lucy all came directly after me, which looked really tough on paper because, whilst it may have been a fantastic feeling to open the show, the general consensus was that you wanted to be near the bottom of the running order to be memorable. I sung well, but there was a long way to go. What was clear was that even in the second week, the same feedback was coming out of the judges':

'Who was that up there?' Nicole said again. 'I'll take your cheeseburger as long as it means something.'

Gary could see that once the music started that I was in my element, but when it was over the nerves returned at a pace. I was able to get lost in the moment, but unable to deal with it and make sense of it all.

Then Louis added, 'You gave it everything…a bit too much?' What did that actually mean? Then, after a pause, 'But you can sing.'

Then came the cruise ship comment. Somebody got it every year. More to the point, I *had* been a cruise ship singer and there was no shame in that. He then said it was a lazy song choice.

Gary jumped straight in and you could see, even this early in the competition that he took an attack on his acts as one on him: 'There is no need to make you current. You are perfect as you are.'

He got instantly who I was trying to be. Myself.

Dermot asked me what I made of the comments and I simply replied that 'it doesn't bother me now...it goes right over my head.' Watching it back amidst all that evident anxiety, I am surprised that they were my words, but I meant what I said and I think of how it all seemed like a pantomime playing out.

By the Sunday night Melanie Masson was on her way home after singing *Never Tear Us Apart* and then *Stay With Me*. District 3 survived but she, despite being a session vocalist with some well-known acts, was no more. I was sad to see her go – we got on really well and she had been like a little Mum to me, but there was a feeling that four of us in this category could not survive and she was the first casualty.

Back at the hotel there was a morbid air. Even though it was every man for himself, the random brutality of the competition had revealed its hand for the second week running.

Little did I know at the time that I had the biggest number of votes – almost a fifth of those of the overall total...and for the second week running. This is why you never find out at the time because it could upset the dynamic of the show. I felt that show business had always got to have an element of smoke and mirrors.

In the days that followed the knives came out.

Chapter Fifteen

I was branded a fake. The papers were slaughtering me. They had picked up on the phrase from my audition that I had 'never put [my] self out there' and was so terrified of public performing that it took me five years to pluck up the courage to audition. I was labelled disingenuous after Mollie Daley from Peel Entertainment, who had hired me on a First Choice Ship in 2000, claimed that I had months of vocal coaching.

I felt for the first time that the tide was turning – that maybe this had come from within. To me, it seemed like too much of a coincidence that Louis had been dropping in the cruise ship remarks. Of course, I had put myself out there before. I had just never put myself out anywhere near *here* before. There was a difference between doing nightly performances in the middle of the ocean and doing a one-off audition for one of the biggest TV shows in the country. Now, that cruise ship comment had legs. With that came mockery and an undercurrent that I was now a liar.

It was ridiculous and only the beginning. I was pissed off, but it was not about to tip me over the edge.

Week Three was to be Club Classics week. JLS – more alumni from the show – and Labrinth with Emeli Sandé were the musical guests. She, in particular had a massive 2012.

I was to sing *Waiting for a Star to Fall* – the one hit wonder from Boy Meets Girl. It had been a smash hit around the world in 1989, but it certainly was not a dance floor anthem. In the mid Noughties, it got remixed with a beat behind it and suddenly became a contemporary disco hit.

For the first time, I was not overjoyed with the song choice, and I did not like the paraphernalia that they were lining up for me on the night. Worse – I was opening the show. I just felt this had bad vibes written all over it, and I felt that the running order might influence voting patterns too.

I also felt that I was being marginalised in the group song that we would all sing together. It seemed that without fail, the main vocals would go to Ella, James and Jahmene.

My instinct was that my song was not Gary's choice. And I think he thought me standing on a podium flanked by dancers for the first time just was not me. It looked...cruise ship.

The comments that followed:

'Who doesn't love a warm cheese toastie?' Nicole revisited her theme. 'It's hard to criticise you.' Then seemed to struggle to find the right words.

Louis said it had been a difficult week for me – presumably a reference to a press mauling. Tulisa then showed her hand: 'It's official for me...It's too cheesy. Rylan is *Babybel*, you're churning your own Stilton.'

She aimed her criticism in Gary's direction. 'It's not fun for me. I don't get it.'

But Gary did. Inside out. He knew exactly the brand he was trying to create, even though it was off message with this choice. 'You are the people's choice.' He coined a great phrase. 'Liverpool is right behind you.'

Nobody was writing his words. And they were perfect.

The fatigue I felt at the cheese comments and Tulisa's dismissal were all that was ringing in my ears when Dermot thrust the microphone my way. I began to shake again.

A few days later, the whole landscape of the competition changed. We all went out for Rylan's birthday and I took the opportunity to confront Tulisa.

'What have I done to upset you? I am trying my best,' I asked.

'Chris, I just don't get you,' she replied then walked away.

But this was nothing compared to what would follow. It was really the last we saw of Lucy.

Chapter Sixteen

It is now Week Four. Halloween Week. Robbie Williams Week.

I had just arrived back in Liverpool when the phone rang.

'Hi Chris, where are you?'

It was Gary in London...

'I'm in Liverpool...I have just got here.'

I was so pleased to be home, for what I thought was some much needed rest, but now I was panicked.

'But it's the masterclass now.'

All the other contestants were waiting. Robbie was in the building.

I was distraught. My relationship with the show was that if they wanted me to jump three foot in the air, I would double it. I was always prepared to do everything and more to be the best and keep them happy.

I asked Gary if I should come back to London, but he said, 'Let's leave it.' I felt shocked and bewildered. Was this some kind of genuine mistake or something else?

'I'm really sorry,' was all I could say.

He told me not to worry, but seemed understandably unhappy. I had only set up my Twitter after Judges' Houses. I was that unprepared for what lay ahead, when many of the other contestants had been honing their identity for months and years. Many of the put downs and snide remarks, when accumulated, meant they could easily be passed off as fact. Some members of the public would take that cruise ship soundbite and regurgitate it on social media, so that you didn't just have a minute's worth of grief from the judges on the live show, you got it all week from people repeating over and over.

I had never really considered this impact, but the accusation about putting myself out there, judges' comments, and the cockup over the masterclass got to me. I was down and lonely and felt that I was losing myself.

By the Saturday of the live show, I managed to have my masterclass session with Robbie, but unfortunately it wasn't televised.

And Robbie was superb with me. I thought he was a brilliant showman, and I got to see him perform *Candy* from the back of the stage, even though it was a pre-record.

I turned up for rehearsal. Gary told me to take the ridiculous eye-liner off. Unfortunately, he had virtually no say in the stage design so, when I walked out to sing the Cutting Crew song, I emerged with a ship behind me. My hair was a mess, as it had begun to fall out with the stress, and once again, I was dressed in a big coat. I looked hideous. And, I can't help but think that making me stand in front of a big ship was no coincidence. It felt like they were taking the absolute piss.

For some reason, they *kept* putting me in coats. This was showbiz, and I looked like I was going to a football match in the winter. To me, it was like they were now labelling me old, along with cruise singer.

The judges didn't seem to have anything specific to say:

'Hi sweetie, that was fun,' Nicole began. 'I wanna give you a hug.'

Louis said they were looking for a future recording star and that I was future cabaret or panto. For some reason I just replied, 'thank you'.

Then the row erupted:

'I am going to stop having a go at you...' Tulisa started, '...and start having a go at Gary. How many of these 80s classics are you going to keep letting him destroy?'

There was a pause.

By now, amidst all this, what I can only describe as, pantomime, I had my own message. I played it humble, but meant it too, trotting out that I was, 'staying true to myself and the people who had voted me in'. Inside, I wanted the stage to swallow me up. I felt awkward and awful. I did not know whether to laugh or cry. All confidence was lost. Today, I recognise that this was the point everything started to go downhill.

After the constant cruise ship comments, and an actual ship in my stage design, I felt like everyone was conspiring against me. When the *Xtra Factor* aired on ITV2 after the main show, most of the viewers were asking why I was still in the competition or why I was in it at all. It was all negative and mainly aimed at me. Louis was asked at one point who the biggest diva was backstage, and he answered, without hesitation, that it was me.

In recent times, programmes like this are often cited for 'now having a duty of care' for the contestants, even though the lure of fame is meant to counter balance as a carrot. It felt to me that all they really cared about was viewing figures, and one or two casualties along the way was acceptable losses. Everything was getting to me. If I had performed well then it seemed as though the other judges would always just talk about the staging or the costume. Every week seemed to follow the same tone and only Gary concentrated on the vocal. My confidence would rise through my performance, but then plummet at the social media fall out.

It was the beginning of my mental breakdown.

Jade Ellis left the competition that week.

She was not the only one to depart. The next day it was announced that Lucy Spraggan had also left the competition.

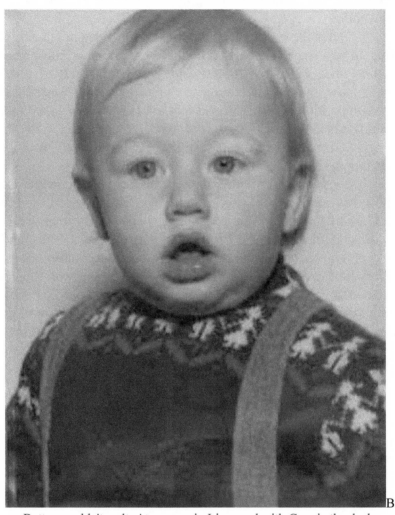
B

Butter wouldn't melt. At nursery in Liverpool with Googie the duck.

Early days – Me and my Gary.

Nan filming *X Factor* in London.

With Gary Barlow, in his dressing room at the Liverpool Philharmonic.

Hitting the arenas for the *X Factor* tour.

Jahméne, James, Rylan and myself on ITV's *This Morning*.

At my Nan's, with Gary and Nan!

Nicole and I at 10 Downing Street, turning on the Christmas lights.

The old work colleagues at LMH.

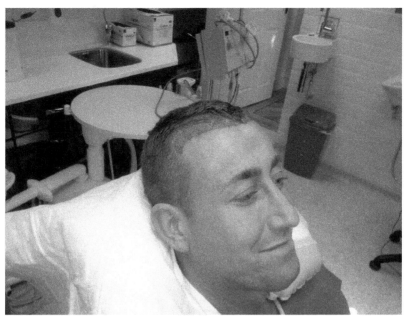

Botched hair transplant.

Danniella Westbrook, my sister, Tricia and niece, Lois, backstage at my first panto.

Bruce Jones from Corrie (Les Battersby) at the opening of my Liverpool Academy.

Gary Barlow, Nick Grimshaw from Radio 1, and myself at the BBC.

Kylie!

Mum and I in the tattoo parlour – first time around!

At the 02 in London, with Niall from One Direction.

Just months before we lost her, with Paul O'Grady and Cilla.

Rita Ora live on the *X Factor*

The last arena gig – wearing other people's costumes! Me and District 3.

David is dead. David is not dead.

My Gary and I on a horse and cart in Central Park, New York, doing a *Sex in the City* scene.

With Jane McDonald at one of her sell-out shows.

My first panto as Prince Charmming with Danniella Westbrook and Lynne Mcgranger (Irene from *Home and Away).*

Chapter Seventeen

On 3 November 2012, it was announced that she had gone. It was very difficult to grasp. In my eyes, she was one of the most unique acts the show had ever seen.

I tweeted, 'I am so sorry to hear you left the competition. I really hope you get better soon. My love and prayers are with you.'

I have no idea whether Lucy would have gone on to win, but with her gone, it seemed like a huge loss. But the show had to go on, and that meant Gwen Stefani rocked up for Week Five with James Arthur given one of her songs and each of us getting about 45 minutes with the No Doubt star. She was lovely.

I was now for the first time scheduled as the last to perform on the show, which I considered an advantage. I do not know how I got there, but it was often perceived as a place where the big hitters performed. Gary had given me Eric Carmen's, *All By Myself,* a massive song, which I loved and I knew I could deliver well, but I did think that it was perhaps the wrong choice for that week.

I didn't really want to sing it, but I had the 'diva' comment still rattling around my head, and I knew that if I objected then that would snowball. We were also extremely late in rehearsal one night, and I just asked if we could go home because I was knackered, looking haggard and feeling utterly used up.

I didn't really think this would count against me. But diva had legs.

I told myself that I needed to confront Louis about this comment. I mean, for Heaven's sake Rylan was on the same show folks! He was a fabulous diva (and always lovely to me)! But now suddenly diva was everywhere. When people get wind that there might be someone acting live a diva in their ranks then they start to see it even when it is not there – in the slightly look or gesture, comment or joke. On their exit,

District 3 later said that they respected me for standing firm against the backlash coming my way, saying booing me was 'really rude' and that I was a 'genuinely nice guy'. They tried to kill the diva story by saying it was just untrue.

I didn't really want to be in the papers – certainly not for that reason. You may well read this now several years on and think, 'Hang on a minute, I have seen Maloney in the papers for all sorts of nonsense, don't tell me he does not court this fame', but see the comment in the context of then. If a judge said it, a troll repeated it and a newspaper wrote it. Therefore, it became fact. And by Week Five it was starting to get out of control and I was the only one taking incoming fire. The seeds of what was to follow were planted here.

By the time I had finished singing one of the great tear-jerkers of all time, I had all but broken down myself on stage.

So, of course, I am on the brink all through the song, and at its end, Nicole asks:

'Why are you crying?'

All I could think of to respond was that I had put everything into it.

She told me that I had hit the money notes and then that it was like an 'eagle's wings that spreads into slow motion'. I'm not sure what that meant. 'Two words,' she continued. 'Major.' I waited for a second word, but none came.

Louis then said:

'We're looking for someone who is going to sell records internationally. I feel like I am in a time machine and I am going back in time'.

Then the shock of the night for me:

'I loved it.' It was Tulisa. 'Brilliant performance…'

I could not believe it.

But then she added, 'Five weeks too late.'

Then she turned to Gary, telling him that it had taken this long to get me to this stage, and that he had finally realised the production was not working.

'Enormous,' Gary shouted. 'You know you are delivering to your public…week after week.'

Amidst all the distractions, Gary was the right mentor and, even though I just wanted to sing, it is definitely true that we had our market and we were going for it. He never once lost that focus.

Then Louis shrugged, as if confused, and said, 'the public voted for him [me]'.

I was safe again. Rylan was in the bottom two. He was now clearly defined as the novelty act, but was a nice guy and, in my eyes, the only other truly diverse dimension left post Lucy. Kye was next to go. I don't suppose it would've worked to have two Overs in the final and, even though I didn't really know it, I had the numbers on my side.

Chapter Eighteen

I felt utterly humiliated.

My nerves at my audition were nothing to what I now felt. They were shot to pieces, but I *couldn't* quit. The public had spent their money on me to get me this far. It would be wrong.

Then another story ended up in the press, saying I 'had lost the plot', after an executive had supposedly called my behaviour, 'unacceptable' for turning up late to rehearsals. I had not been late and that conversation did not even happen. There were way too many opinions and half-truths at play here. Addressing each of them was exhausting.

Next, I am shown a copy of the *Daily Star,* where Rylan – possibly my best friend in the group – is saying there is 'substance' in the diva rumour, claiming that I pushed in front of him at a Kim Kardashian meet and greet, and stating that he is the same person he was at the start of the contest, and that he didn't need a sob story or to be rude to get where he wanted. I have no doubt in my mind that Rylan either did not say any such thing at all, or that it was just said as a joke to wind everyone up. Whichever, I found that it was now being perpetuated as a truth.

It seemed that even that weekend's guests piled in. It was a Best of British weekend, and Ed Sheeran, One Direction and the previous year's winners, Little Mix, were all on the bill.

The latter took to Twitter and dubbed me Christopher *Maphoney,* and the subsequent *The Sun* article, stating that nobody would buy my records if I won. That felt like a particularly harsh betrayal, considering their roots with the show. The article also stated that I had spent thousands of my own money phoning to vote for myself.

This was clearly bullshit.

I was to open the show that week with Elton John's *I'm Still Standing.* My mind was scrambled.

And you can see it in my performance. It was probably my worst effort on the show. I looked ridiculous and knew it too. I entered the stage in the now habitual coat. I just didn't understand why they insisted in dressing me in a coat. Around me, I am fighting for stage space with dancers in something resembling gym suits and skiwear-like glasses. There was no synergy between us, so the gap made me look ancient. You lost your head in the choreography, but my mind was long since starting to go.

At the end of the song, all I could think was, what the fuck was that? I got the camera angles wrong, I got the dance moves wrong and worst of the three – the ultimate sin – I got the words wrong. When I knew I was messing up, I just mumbled.

I was waiting for a mauling.

'I like your confidence…a little nervous, a little lacklustre,' Nicole began.

'You are the karaoke king,' she condemned me. 'We are looking for an artist to break new boundaries.'

When you hear a judge use the karaoke word, there is almost no way back.

Louis repeated it and then said that watching me every week was like listening to *Heart FM.*

'Are people voting for you gonna buy it? Tulisa added.

It seemed that she was now questioning my future prospects, not just my performance on the night.

'It is a best of British weekend,' she continued.

I couldn't help myself, and heard myself say, 'Elton John is the best British, I have heard.'

Her comments had been cutting previously, but these really pissed me off. Ever the amazing mentor, Gary had the last word:

'You shocked me. This has been a massive week for you.'

The truth was that of all the weeks to criticise me this was actually the one. I accept that I was crap. But Dermot had picked up on one thing:

'You're in the hottest studio…and you're always wearing coats.'

Now, Dermot is a smart man, and he knew that I did not turn up dressed in a coat of my own accord. Perhaps he could see the ridiculousness of it, I don't know. I was never dressed in the coat again after that.

The bottom two came down to Union J and District 3. As is often the way, by this stage in the competition, there really was not room for both of them. There was not much room for me, despite this sixth consecutive week (out of six) in which I had won the vote.

The fact of the matter is that, somehow, despite my deteriorating health and becoming a virtual recluse, I was still in the driving seat.

Chapter Nineteen

Week Seven. Reality check. James Arthur seems like he is not even in the running for this competition. I am meant to be preparing for Guilty Pleasures Week. Instead, I am now spending almost every moment distracted and depressed by the sideshow and that is the internet effect.

The lies and half-truths get out there and then social media runs with it and lazy journalism finds its non-story, so you spend the next five days trying to extinguish a non-storm about nothing to do with the aspiration and dreams of why you entered.

Of course, they do say that there is no such thing as bad publicity.

In my mind, it felt like the programme revelled in the slaughtering of the sacrificial lamb, when programmes like *Strictly* never seem to need to resort to such gimmicks. I can't dance for toffee, but that is a show I would love to do.

The result of all the put downs, media bias, lies and half-truths meant that I was now being trolled on a regular basis. My Twitter knowledge was months young. I was not wise to any of this. Naively, I did not realise that you might wake up on a Monday, having made it through another week, to find hundreds of messages calling you every name under the sun and questioning your whole self-worth.

You can't really reply either – diva at play who can't take the criticism is the inevitable fall-out. Plus, suddenly if you respond to keyboard warriors, you make another story about a story that was not a story in the first place. You then only have yourself to blame. You fuel the fire.

The media were already going to town on this, reporting that I had received death threats. They told *The Mirror:*

'The welfare of our contestants is our key priority and we work with them to provide what support is needed.'

Among the crackers I received:

'You don't deserve this baloney! Kill yourself.'

'I'll hunt Maloney down and kill him.'

The problem is that you are already in such a low place that there is nowhere else to go, but you then drag your family into it, who are 250 miles away, and are already making the trip up every week at their own expense, yet helpless to help *you* during the week. Because they love you, they understandably share the attack as though it is personal attack on them.

So, by the time I came to perform Bonnie Tyler's *Total Eclipse of the Heart,* I really was losing the concept of the dream and barely hanging on to my sanity. The surreal nature of the show meant nothing compared to what was going on in real life.

I had almost tuned out by the time Nicole called me 'creepy', adding it was 'a lot to take in', but concluded it was 'nice'. Her comments felt mean, obscure and then confused.

Louis said:

'You must be doing something right,' but then added, 'I dunno what it is.'

Tulisa seemed resigned:

'I admit defeat. You sounded really good.'

Gary said that all they had to comment on was what was going on behind me, but that I was a fantastic guy, but all I wanted was to get off the stage and forget the whole thing. Their words no longer resonated with me – I was numb – but I knew what they said would now have repercussions on social media almost immediately. Reading some of that stuff and people's twists on it outside the cauldron of live performance was much harder coming from faceless strangers than the obscure panto of the judges' table. The trolls might get to me, but the judges would no more.

When Dermot came to me for my reaction, I gave the only answer I could think of: I wished my sister a Happy Birthday live on air.

That was a small moment, but a massive one too, in showing people that I loved my roots and my family, and most importantly, above all else, that I now finally knew that this was all bollocks and that, in the long run, I knew what really mattered.

It did not stop things getting a whole lot worse.

Chapter Twenty

Dermot arrived to take me for a walk. I had never heard of anything like this happening before. What was he doing here inviting me for a chat?

'How are you doing?' he asked.

It felt like genuine concern, not orchestrated in any way.

We went for a long, long stroll. He could see that I was shaking all the time, and I told him I really didn't like confrontation. By now, the shaking was greater. It had just crept up and up into what was now full on anxiety and depression. He told me simply that I had to fight back.

In terms of the show, he may have been right, but that shooting shining star on the horizon was dwindling out. I really knew that I was struggling to keep it together, and that was actually nothing to do with the performance.

I wasn't therefore too convinced that his words would help, as lovely as it was of him to tell them to me. By the time Saturday came, I was charged with *Fernando* and *Dancing on the Ceiling* in Abba and Motown week.

I felt that is was a mess from start to finish. The state I was in, I got the words wrong again. To me, it felt like they were revelling in my torture.

In fact, you could barely see me. There were around twenty people cavorting on stage like an orgy, which, looking back on it, seemed ridiculous to me. This was a song about two old freedom-fighter friends reminiscing about a battle. But, of all the Abba songs, it was probably the only one I could do.

'That was a lovely theatrical piece,' Nicola said in what I could only interpret as a patronising tone.

'There was definitely something in the air that night. All the guys around you took their tops off. I am just glad you kept your top on,' was Louis's contribution. To me, he looked like he was on his dream night out.

Tulisa reiterated her previous remark, suggesting I was weirdly dangerous in some way, by labelling it 'creepy' with all the swimwear. 'I am trying to stop myself being giggly – the staging is almost funny,' she explained herself.

I felt like they were all suggesting that I had ordered 20 people to dress like that for my own benefit or to enhance the song in some vague way.

'Another great performance,' Gary valiantly managed. 'Sorry about those comments.'

Louis turned on Gary, saying it was Gary's fault, that he was trying to pull the wool over everyone's eyes.

I really did think it was all so stupid that I must be going home. It was hard enough anyway to evaluate your own performance so soon after you have delivered it, but the events of the week just clouded every vision I had.

And right after I had sung, Louis Tomlinson posted on Twitter:

'Christopher Maloney showing his nasty side, no sympathy whatsoever. He has to go tomorrow!'

I have no idea where this came from. One Direction had been brilliant to me the previous week. Again, I say it's hard not to feel like there was some kind of conspiracy going on.

Lucy Spraggan tweeted that she couldn't wait to see 'my lovely boys' and then listed everyone except me. Ella, who had gone the previous Sunday retweeted it. I do not know where that came from either.

By the time I had performed my second song, and Lionel Richie had sent a message of support, I was so out of it that it almost meant nothing at all. The negativity was drowning me. Not even a superstar like that could drag this cruise ship singer out of the murky depths.

This was though, a better performance and I loved dancing behind the audience and going in amongst them for the first time. Unfortunately, Tulisa did not turn around, but remained staring straight at the stage. She could only say that she didn't always believe me and that there was a disconnect.

Louis Walsh condemned me for being Blackpool or Benidorm karaoke material. But Nicole's comments were even more cutting, though difficult to comprehend:

'You tried something new. I am more of a *Coco Pops* girl drowning in full fat milk. You are giving me vanilla skimmed-free milk on top of a cornflake, like a single cornflake. I'm looking for soul and I don't see much soul there.'

I'm not sure how anyone could consider that constructive feedback.

As Gary rightly pointed out, it was not an emotional song. He said he was uncomfortable with the comments. Rightly so – to me, they felt empty and meaningless.

I simply told Dermot that I was staying true to myself and the people who voted for me, and he told me that I said that every week. I think that was him reminding me of the conversation we had a few days previously.

Against the odds, I had done enough though to survive. I did so with mixed emotions. Special guest Bruno Mars told me to keep up the good work. It felt then that maybe that's just what everyone says. Rylan went home this time, which I was sad about, but I think he felt it was time to go. And with him went my last real ally, beyond Gary.

Chapter Twenty-One

Janette Galbraith sold a story about me. Of all the times for someone to come out of the woodwork – well, obviously, yes of all the times – just before the semi-final.

The press wrote that I was the 'bookies' favourite'. It's funny that they had never mentioned that before. They had said I was a diva who missed a masterclass, and Louis Tomlinson and Little Mix were gunning for me, but never any mention before that I was any kind of favourite. Until it suited them.

For their story to sell as many papers as possible, it meant they had to position me higher in order for some nobody to take me down. They had belittled me at every juncture, but if that was the case, why even bother running the story. And therein lies their game.

So, you may recall that I had been on the cruise ship with Galbraith. And for whatever reason – nose out of joint at my early promotion, or whatever – she felt aggrieved.

Well, she had certainly waited for her moment, storing it up for years. I do not know where she got the photo from, as she was in it and, nobody took selfies back in those days, but she ran to the national press and told them that I had tried to strangle her on the MSC Lirica cruise ship in the Mediterranean! I loved the fact that the article labelled her a 'professional singer' – insinuating that I wasn't, and then went on to claim that we were both the lead singers, which, I think, was exactly the focus of her jealousy.

She claimed that I snapped on Christmas Eve 2005, during an argument about me bringing someone back to the cabin we shared, that we trashed the bathroom, and that she told me what everyone else thought of me.

I apparently flipped and grabbed her around the throat. I am having to google this as my memory has a gap here! She says that she ran and cried and was urged to report it and then didn't turn up for the Christmas Day lunch the next day. She claims that I was told to leave the ship and that she was in a terrible state.

I ask one question: why is this the first I hear of this? I look at the date. Oh, the semi-final is looming. What an uncanny coincidence.

I rolled my eyes at how low people would go. It still came as a bit of a surprise. It is so hard to explain, but you get into a mindset where you actually expect something every week. But you would never know what it would be or when it would rear its ugly head, but by the very left-field nature of it, it couldn't help but stress you out even more. I certainly did not see this coming. I struggled to recall her name when I started reading the article. It was way down the league table of damage, compared to some of the stuff that was going on. But it still left me exhausted. You weigh it up and flashback to what actually happened, and then you second-guess the sickly, vindictive conversations that must have gone on between Galbraith and the paper, and that level of cunning planning is almost as bad as the piece itself. And yet, there is no comeback. You complain and that is now a story. You refer it to the press complaints people and they all regulate themselves!

The *Guardian* also ran a piece entitled 'When you invent a show any fool can win, you can't moan if they do' and stated that I *would* be voted out of the competition this week – but only if the show had its way. But of course, it slated my character too, comparing me to a puppet, a quivering chicken nugget, and having a devastating honk, describing me as a joke act and a gran-pleaser, and that an insider had already said that I would be dropped from the record label if I won, rounding off with, that if I did succeed, it would be fitting punishment for the label. Everybody, it seemed had an opinion in this matter – except the public, who just kept on voting.

I retired to my room, shattered and not really wishing to engage. I had been working from 7 am to midnight most days. The producers actually told me to take some down time. I was grateful.

120

I hit the sack. Then there was a knock on the door.

I had five minutes to get ready.

I stunk. My hair was falling out in the sink, even more so than ever before. I had four and a half minutes to get nowhere near ready. The limo was waiting for me at the back of the hotel.

We are driving into the centre of London. It is all traffic lights and a haze of Christmas shopping to me. Then we make a sharp turn and suddenly are at the back of 10 Downing Street. I really could've used a bit more notice. I looked a state and a half.

What the hell am I doing here? A few moments before, I was dozing on the bed, reflecting on Galbraith, trolls, and oh yes, this week's performance, as if that hardly mattered. Now, I am shaking the Prime Minister, David Cameron's hand.

What the hell is going on?

Outside, the press were gathered and a choir was ready to go… But, in the back of my mind, I also recognised the moment for what it was. This was Downing Street and a chance to get some good press, and when David Cameron took to the mic, with Nicole standing next to him, well, frankly it was like a scene from *Love Actually*. It really was something and nothing, because realistically it was a press shoot, not the lighting up of Number 10's Christmas Tree. The public couldn't get down that street anyway, so the only people who *were* there were the press. It was purely a media exercise for everyone. I just went along with the spin.

By Saturday, I knew I could be in serious trouble. The songs were supposed to be 'songs for you' and 'songs to get you to the final'. For me, it meant Josh Groban's, *You Raise Me Up* and Michael Buble's, *Haven't Met You Yet.* The latter had a red flag next to it. I loved Buble, but if I messed it up, I was definitely going home.

That was all I was thinking. There was no vision on my part that, if I got through this weekend, I was in the final. It had all become a treadmill and a haze. There was no light at the end of the tunnel. Physically surviving the experience had surpassed surviving the public vote.

On stage for *You Raise Me Up,* I was now permanently in a suit. Since the coat comment, they had dressed me better. When I hit the bridge of the song, a huge choir of about 50 appeared on stage. The audience went crazy and I knew I had delivered.

For once, I ended the song with a smile. Only Gary stood to applaud.

'You've earned your place,' Nicole conceded. 'I would love it if I could feel your performance.'

I just thought, 'piss off' but said nothing.

Within me, I had found some brittle, but I still couldn't blurt it out to their faces.

'That was a great Westlife song,' Louis said, when everyone knew it was really a Josh Groban track, before promising me that Andrew Lloyd Webber was going to call and that he could see me in the West End.

At this point, I just thought, 'what bullshit'. And that, in my eyes, it was his way of accepting that I was doing well by switching from cruise ship to another musical genre.

Andrew Lloyd Webber never called by the way. I am still waiting.

Surprisingly, Tulisa said she really enjoyed it, but I didn't really feel any emotion from her. Then Dermot brought up what had happened backstage, which none of the public knew or would understand the reference to.

'You mentioned Westlife four times in one link,' he told Louis. 'I don't know what you have done, but Christopher's Nan is after you.'

I was shocked that Dermot mentioned it on air, but felt it was a major victory.

Then I had to do Buble – the song I was dreading. Rightly so. Nicole said it was not my strongest performance and that was true. Gary said they were trying to showcase who I was going to be, and that I was an artist in the same genre, and that he knew people were going to be voting for me. Tulisa could only remind everyone that I had a big fanbase. Louis berated Gary for picking the wrong song, before curiously adding that 'he loved my first song and he loved all those 80s power ballads with the key changes' – exactly the songs I had been singing every week that he had been slating me for.

Despite the Buble aberration, I was stunned to survive and sad to see Union J go home. I had made it through to the final. I was there.

I really had made it!

Only James Arthur, Jahmene and myself remained. The release of tension was massive – and it was exactly that. The thought that I could go home finally as the last show was to be in Manchester was as massive as getting there itself. I knew it was a colossal achievement but all the other pressures were now so great that a change of scenery, getting out of that hotel and heading back up north meant *as* much. Managing the anxiety was the most important issue, because that could stay with me forever. Being in the final three was just a moment in time.

Before I could pack up in London, I had to pick up a few more pieces. Union J were suddenly in the press issuing a 'public warning' that a victory to me could damage the show's reputation.

And what the hell did that mean? Surely, for the show, it was the same old same old. I suddenly felt like whoever had left at the weekend would have slated me, regardless. There had not been any animosity just 48 hours before. This week of all weeks was not the one to get dragged into non-stories, but I wasn't the only one unhappy.

On the Tuesday we had to record the winner's song, a track called *The Reason*.

I had never heard it before in my life. They would play me a verse of the original then I would listen and record it. This could be the biggest moment of my life and I was having to learn and record it on the fly. It felt terribly rushed to me. And my voice was failing me.

I could not have been more relieved to get the hell out of London and head towards Manchester.

I was petrified of having to sing it and not really knowing the words. Plus, I could barely speak. I went straight to the doctor when I got home. He could see there was something wrong and confirmed:

I was on the brink of a nervous breakdown.

Yet I still had a multitude of interviews to do. One minute I was on Radio 1 with Nick Grimshaw, and the next I was on breakfast TV. I decided to make a small protest, wearing a sign saying, 'On Voice Rest'. I really was at the end of the line.

It was relentless. I had to do one of those homecoming gigs at the Empire Theatre in Liverpool. Radio City gave away their allocation of tickets in 25 seconds. Gary would perform with me in the run up to Saturday's final.

It was all part of the of the show, and that included filming me on a ferry across the Mersey. The weather was appalling and I was disappointed that there was no audience. I just wanted it over.

I just felt like the whole week was a blur, from recording the winner's song, to giving interviews, to performing on a ferry.

The song that is supposed to win me the show is Irene Cara's *Flashdance*.

Gary politely said that I had gone out there and smashed it, and maybe I had because you can only take on the song you had been given. It was lovely of him.

I knew I was not going to win and so did my family.

My anxiety had really come full circle too, re-appearing through the physical discomfort of losing my voice. I really did not feel equal in any way.

I was now so consumed with suspicion that when Jahmene's mic did not work during his performance, I thought that – ironically – it was a set up. I thought that they could easily have run on the stage with a spare, but they left it, leaving the judges to say 'what a pro he had been'. I don't know, maybe it was just an unlucky blip. On the night, I saw it as some sort of reverse psychology to make people say how well he had coped – star quality and a true pro.

It left me with one chance to turn it around. Nicole was singing with both Jahmene and James, so in my desperation, I thought that might fatigue Nicole.

I knew – as much as he was my idol and I was in awe of him – that I couldn't go wrong singing with Gary.

He could play it blind and give me a nod and a wink. It felt like Gary was getting dragged into my nightmare. It seemed like everyone wanted to see us as an old pair who sung old classics in cardigans to people in nursing homes.

I knew I had blown it. Perhaps, I peaked too soon. Maybe I wasn't as good towards the end or, possibly the relentless stories about my character had re-positioned me from a nervous emotional wreck that the public liked, to one that they had had enough of.

It didn't matter and I didn't care. I was shattered beyond exhaustion, and after the *Xtra Factor,* I went back to my room and just broke down. I shook a million times worse than at my audition. I sobbed uncontrollably all night. You have to understand that this had nothing to do with the performance or the likely outcome. It was the beginning of a full-blown breakdown.

Somehow, *my* Gary got me through the night and tomorrow was another day.

Except, it was a whole lot darker.

Chapter Twenty-Two

It was left to Jahmene and James to fight it out. I had been voted out.

My dream was over and even though I told the *Xtra Factor* that it was just the beginning and Gary was dubbing me 'The Maloney', I was not so sure that there was a fresh start around the corner.

In fact, I was that poorly that I really couldn't even think straight at all. I mean, who realistically can announce themselves, with any certainty, to the world on live TV minutes after they have been eliminated, that in effect, you ain't see nothin' yet, and the best is yet to come?

I just wanted to get off that stage and into my bed, and the next morning (the Sunday) getting out of it would be the only challenge.

In my terrible state, my paranoia went into overdrive.

I left and went back to my room, sobbing again for the rest of the afternoon.

This was a tipping point. My recollection of that day is almost non-existent. Every minute rolled into the next one, without me being aware of the time.

Of course, I did not watch the final show. It was only later that I learned that James had won, obviously. My fractured mind was occupied elsewhere. Within no time at all, it had appeared online that *I* had pulled out of the show after turning up full of booze, had hit the roof at rehearsal after being only given one line in the medley, that I risked losing my lucrative place on the tour, and that I had in fact showed up for the final in the end but nobody wanted me there.

I had no idea where it could have come from, but I was too busy suffocating into a black hole of depression.

Home was the only place to be in times like this, with the people who had been on the ride with you, who also hadn't changed a jot whilst all around them had. I spent the Sunday night in the arms of my Mum and awoke on the Monday staring into the abyss.

I did not know what lay ahead and I am not talking about the shattered pieces of a possible career. I was barely functioning minute to minute.

Somewhere in London, though, an alarm bell was ringing. I am not sure if a lone dissenting voice suddenly spoke up, but I received a call from one of the big wigs on the show.

The Carolynne Poole non-story had also now hit the press.

'After ten weeks, the mask came off. It was like he couldn't keep it up any more,' she had whinged about me.

Then Kye piled in, saying, I had been shown for who I really was! I think I was realising that they had been shown for who *they* really were! It felt like just another ploy to gain column inches as, over the coming weeks, the publicity would ultimately die down.

The exec asked me if everything was OK, and I told him straight.

No, it wasn't.

'All these stories are making me worse... suicidal... they have got to stop,' I cried down the phone at him.

She was not the only one to depart. The next day it was announced that Lucy Spraggan had also left the competition.

He told me that he was sending a doctor – a lady called Marci from The Priory clinic, who would drive through the night to help me. It felt like some sort of admission and it seemed like it was coming from high up. He could have got somebody more junior to make that call, and it seemed they already had the medic on standby. With all the stress contestants are under, this kind of scenario must have been brewing for years, but only now when somebody actually stood up and said 'he is on the brink' the gears were put in motion. You may guess what follows:

The nurse arrived on the Tuesday. She told me that she could take me for help now, or I could stay amongst my family, but advised the latter might be best. I told her that the stories about me had broken me. It was true. I was having a nervous breakdown.

I got prescribed some medication, but never saw that nurse again.

Gary Barlow was almost the only person to stay in touch. He told me to keep my head down, not rise to the bait, and that one day I would have my say. That he made contact at all meant more than any words, but he was right, of course.

Foolishly, I later tried to tell my side of the story, but only encountered doors slammed in my face. I am sure that I was not thinking straight, but my mindset must have been that it was time to do what everyone had done to me. Of course, nobody wanted the other side of the story, nor did they want Gary Barlow dragged into it.

Stupidly, I had a couple of obligations to the show still to fulfil and somehow, through a haze, managed to attend. I was very much on autopilot and nowhere near well enough to do so. One of these was the G-A-Y gig that was important to me; another I simply felt I could not cancel: paying a surprise visit just a few days before Christmas to a group of nurses from the Royal Liverpool Hospital at their festive do.

Beyond that, I was rarely seen, except in an article that confirmed that I would be joining the traditional tour in 2013. I think me confirming so was just a moment of face-saving pride. I did not want to let the people down who had voted for me, but I also did not want to roll over and let them win. To have pulled out would have been to concede.

The truth was that when I woke on New Year's Day, I was still broken, eating little and rarely surfacing. The calendar had stood still. I was living in *Groundhog Day,* with no light at the end of the tunnel. My shakes were terrible and almost continual. I rarely washed. I had no choice but to stay at Mum's. My mind had been attacked and my body had shut down.

There was only one dot on the landscape that gave me some focus and something to aim at, and that, unbelievably, was the tour, where I would be re-united with so many of the people who had apparently had a pop at me.

I can't say I was trying to get myself ready, because it is not something you can do when your mind has gone. But the closer it was, the more I was woken from my trance and, by mid-January, I think fear dragged me back to some sort of acceptable state, and I was able to draw one conclusion – that if I didn't do it, it would have all been for nothing.

I felt that the one positive element before I joined the fourteen-date trek around the country was that it was not run by the TV company, but a completely different organisation. That calmed my nerves slightly, though I was still running on empty, functioning halfway between autopilot and anti-depressants. Then the call came in that I was needed for rehearsals in London. The tour would start in Manchester on 27 January, and I would sing *All By Myself, I'm Still Standing, Flashdance,* and *You Raise Me Up.*

Even though I had said yes, I told them that I was still unsure about it. The press were back on the case too, with 'he's doing it, he's not doing it.' Then I realised it was an absolute necessity. The deadline focussed the brain. Something lifted in me. There was still a massive cloud hanging over me, but it was raining a little less. Saying yes and heading to London really was my first trip over to the light side in close to a month.

We began in Manchester and concluded a month later in Belfast, taking in most of the major cities in the UK.

I actually got to know some of the acts really for the first time. James came out of his shell a little now that the pressure was off. Yet still controversy followed not far behind.

One night a security guard for the tour assaulted me. Outside the hotel there were loads of fans banging on the door, and nobody was doing anything about it, so I went to get help and knocked on our minder's room, only to find him in bed with a girl. He flipped and grab me by the throat. I managed to get away from him, but was badly shaken.

130

The next morning, I complained to the tour manager and told him to remove the guy and that I would not continue if he remained – exactly the kind of words that would earn you a diva reputation, of course, but I felt wholly justified in this case.

And it got worse. One female fan was tweeting me relentlessly and her boyfriend lost control, assuming that there was something going on between us. I think it was plain to see to most people that this was unlikely, to say the least, but her boyfriend became obsessive to the point of becoming dangerous. I never replied and, of course, learnt much of the story in catch up – notably, when I turned up at one venue, only to be met by the police, who sat me down and told me that I could not go on stage that night.

Now, for the first time, I did become a diva! I refused to comply. People had paid money to come and see me, I told them.

'There may be a man in the audience with a gun,' they warned. 'He is threatening to shoot you in the head.'

The tour management also agreed – there was no way I was performing. I told *them* straight too. I didn't really know what I was thinking, except I did believe that people had paid their money, and I *must* deliver. I think, I was also in the frame of mind not to be told what to do.

Of course, for one of my songs, I had to head into the audience, and, at that point, I was terrified. My eyes were constantly scanning the crowd, and trying to see through the back of my head. In the end, he kept away that night, and I heard was subsequently arrested. I have no idea how people talk themselves into these situations, where they believe their partner is dating someone off the telly, and then announce they are going to shoot them. It is the kind of thing that happens in America, isn't it? No here.

The tour itself still presented its little politics – as the winner, James got a dressing room to himself. Union J came in with their own management, and were making a film and doing a book, often making demands like kicking us out of *our* dressing room to do so. But credit to them, they were smarter than the rest of us. We had been assigned management by the show, and now had to pay them 20% for the prearranged tour. I wasn't sure what that was all that about? That period of illness had cost me dearly in many ways.

Some people had had time to reflect, and get smart since leaving the show – some had been out for months. Union J had clearly used the time wisely. Still, there were always those little irritations when you're touring with so many diverse personalities.

I was always first on the tour bus – somebody was invariably late, and we would have to wait. There was one day that I was running over by a matter of minutes, though. Unbelievably, they left without me, forcing me to get a train to Scotland, and a taxi from the station to the arena, arriving soaked from torrential rain. I don't know whether it was accidental or being nasty, but it left me angry and upset.

Then I discovered that District 3 had got into my phone. I had around 120,000 followers on Twitter at the time, and they posted that I had just got out of bed with three men. They thought it was just a fun prank to play on me, but to me it was just another example of being made a mockery. They did later apologise – I don't think they realised how hurtful it would be to me.

However, I was glad that I did the tour, and there was more downtime to manage anxiety than there was during the TV show. Press leaks were less, but there still seemed to be some bad vibes lingering. I had partly taken control of my own destiny, in that I had been writing a small column for *Now* magazine, and when you suddenly are writing the words yourself, it changes the landscape. But there were still some vultures out there.

One man, who had consistently lived off *X Factor* and other celebrity stories for years was the Showbiz Editor at *The Sun*, a newspaper to whom you were always careful about what you said, given its historic relationship with Liverpool.

Dan invited me, along with my sister, to go to see him to talk about the column. I thought I was discussing *X Factor* and the tour.

'What does your partner think about you being away?' he suddenly asked.

'Oh, he's fine with it,' I replied. 'And supports me.'

As soon as I said *he,* I was suddenly guilty of deceiving fans! I was never asked about it during the show.

The piece he wrote pitched Dan as the saviour – the man who was one of the first to dub me 'Baloney' and mock me, but claims to have been increasingly worried about me during the final weeks of the show, when the bullying and cyber attacks kicked in.

I would rather not have done it in public for my Dad to have to read about – nor did I think it was supposed to be an issue these days.

I felt that it just reeked of agenda and hypocrisy. From what I understand, Dan Wootton was the go-to man for stories on that show. I believe that he was there most weeks. Every week I had turned up with Gary cheering me on. It was not really a secret or a big deal. So, I'm not sure how Dan missed it all that time, to see my love of Abba and soft furnishings.

I think I needed it to draw a line under all this – except I had no idea what to do next.

I signed to Quest, which was part of Syco. I did not have a lot of options, and it seemed the smart thing to do.

It seemed that few *X Factor* artists had been prolific in the first year out of the show.

I decided to quit. There was no way I wanted to slip into oblivion. That was not what I did this for, and I knew from the votes that I did have a fan base, and had to deliver something for them. As far as I'm away, no Overs entrant had ever really delivered, but the public had done so for me, so I signed to Tristar Records, and told the *Liverpool Echo* that I would definitely not be releasing an album of covers. To me, it seemed that too many previous contestants had gone down that route before.

133

By October, we were ready to release *My Heart Belongs to You.* To get to this stage was fantastic. I felt like a superstar just actually cutting a record. Finally, it was all coming together, and that meant more than anything daft like getting to Number One, which had previously been so important to me.

Ten months previously, at the height of my breakdown, I could not have envisaged getting anywhere close to this. Now, I was here. Before release, I had one small ritual I wanted to complete.

I sent it to Gary Barlow.

'Do not release this song,' he replied. 'I'm gonna be brutal. Do not release this. It is not going to chart and the press will have a field day.'

He thought the track was just alright, sounded a bit dated, and the lyric was old-fashioned.

'I know you want success and this is not the way you will get it.'

But his words arrived too late. I had already signed the contract to release it, and at this stage, almost a year after the show, I was always going to go ahead anyway, even if he was probably right. I think we had a different perspective on the song. He was protecting me from a slaughtering and thought I could do better. I understood that to be even in this position was astonishing, and that, somehow, was almost enough for me. Whether luck or something else, I must have done some small thing right though, as I still get royalties to this day, and later I was approached from Japan (a pretty big pop market) to sign to Fuji Records, who came over and filmed me and were committed to a deal but there was a condition. They needed TV footage of me from *X Factor.* Freemantle, in the UK, refused permission.

I loved the track in fact. But I hated the video. My hair was all over the shop in a crazy pop star way. Whilst I had been concerned on the *X Factor* about how they were trying to create an image for me that became a stereotype – with all the overcoats – this was different. For the very first time, we were working from a blank canvas. A chance to build my own look. I felt, for my first crack at it, I failed completely.

I did love the thrill that, after all the pop videos that I had watched over the years, I was now making one – still slow in the process, but so different from the making of a VT with the TV show, where it all seemed so frantic, to get the edit they wanted and the context they needed.

Overall, I was satisfied. Three years later, I was delighted to storm the Japanese charts. I had finally had a Top 20 hit. Dreams do come true! I knew I still had fans, despite not delivering anything credible up to this point. The numbers week in week out told me that people had spent money voting for me, that they could have better spent elsewhere, and that meant I had a moral obligation to deliver.

I had finally done so.

Chapter Twenty-Three

The year after I left *X Factor* the unexpected happened. Somebody from the Overs category won the show. This must have been great news for the producers, in that it finally ticked that box, and answered those critics who shouted every year that nobody would ever win from that group. But, of course, it must have given them the issue of them automatically being positioned as old – possibly a crooner – which must cause huge problems for marketing that person.

It may not come as a surprise to you that I knew Sam Bailey. You will have also heard that this is a business where everybody knows everybody. I think it is safe to say that if you were of a certain age group, you probably were competing and working with a pool of similar talent to yourself. So, you will not be shocked to learn that Sam Bailey also worked the cruises.

The more I think about it – so many people had taken this route. Why? Because, it was regular work and a chance to see the world – the reality actually was that you saw the ports of the world – and you learnt the craft. Night after night, and every afternoon, you were honing your trade, and others that you didn't know you had. If I wasn't singing I was generally being sociable with the old dears at Bingo. In short, you were cutting it most days a week, but you became a professional partly because you were always around the audience, even if you just went for food or a little break on deck. There is no escape at sea. Unless you jump.

So, Sam Bailey had taken that route, and I got a call early in 2013 – as the 'Overs' person, who had made it the furthest since the first winner, Steve Brookstein, when the category did not even exist yet. I was as close to the mark to anyone watching the show who thought they would have a chance if they entered.

A friend of Sam's rang for advice. It was a ghost from the past! When I had near fatally cut myself on the ship, I had stayed in contact with one of the girls on board, who turned out to know Sam. Her friend, Sam, wanted to apply. Of course, Sam had read stuff about me, and was a mature woman with a family of her own, so the need to run it by someone close to that was greater than if you were a Union J just starting out. When you had the world at your feet, you had nothing to lose. If you are a bit older and have children yourself then that is a scrutiny you have every chance of falling foul of.

Very few people make the live shows from all the contestants. That means a lot of people fail. As a result, few know how you will be received. When I look back, I could have been vilified as the quivering wreck and lambasted for 'using' my Nan.

The truth is that I was in that state and they asked her on to the stage. Plus, luckily, it went my way. The judges (then) and the audience loved me. But, that vulnerability that the public saw on day one and generally supported through votes became a narrative for the show, for Dermot, and even at times for Gary, albeit in his loveable and supportive way. You can see from my story how it could therefore go either way – and did. It was certainly the right thing to do for Sam to enquire about the process.

At the end of the day, I could have screamed, 'don't do it' a thousand times down the phone to her, and this is still something that, especially at that age, makes you say 'sod it, one last chance', and whilst I did encourage her to do the show, she certainly took her opportunity with both hands. But they did give her exactly the same treatment, labelling her as 'cruise ship', which Louis Walsh still seemed to think was a put-down, whereas most people who have worked them see it as earning your stripes. Furthermore, Sam, too, was accused of covering up her cruise ship background. Pitched as 'no real previous experience' (which is nonsense in the Overs, because everyone has tried to make it so many times before), they then accused her of lying about her cruise ship past. What was there to lie about anyway? It didn't matter anyway – I just knew she was going to win. She stormed it, coming first or second every week, and taking over half the vote in the final.

I heard on the grapevine that they were going to do something different for her too – that Gary was going to write the songs for her, and her album would be new material. It turned out to be just a rumour unfortunately.

When she won, I texted her to congratulate her. It was some time later, when things went a bit sour for her, that I heard again from her.

There could have been many reasons for that. It may be that she just got what she needed from me. She was almost definitely very busy. Or perhaps she had so many messages that she just didn't reply. It is a crazy time for all involved, as I knew only too well.

Either way, she won and, perhaps this is my ego talking, but I would like to think that my near success the previous year had helped change the landscape. And hopefully that meant that not just boy or girl bands or youngsters would win in future.

By Mother's Day 2013, I had a chance to record an album, targeted specifically for release at that point in the calendar. I knew that it was the wrong thing to do, and that I was potentially short-changing the public. It wasn't me and I felt that it had no lasting value. By the following day, it would be almost worthless, until twelve months ahead, when they could get another go at it. It was exactly the kind of move that I was afraid of from Syco, going way back as far as Brookstein.

Were covers considered that safe? Why was there this assumption that if somebody currently in the public eye put their spin on a classic that it would come out anything other than worse? There had been some great alternative versions of big songs over the years, and I loved covering *The Rose* for *X Factor,* but an entire album made you a one trick pony, didn't it? I ran the risk of slaughtering people's all-time favourites, and there was a severe danger of becoming a novelty act that might have a couple of hit records and would then disappear into obscurity.

Part of the problem was that I couldn't get on TV to promote anything. Radio was different, and I loved my tours of the stations, especially going up the tower to *Radio City* in Liverpool. I am sure everybody says this at some point, but when you are suddenly being interviewed on air and hearing your own song being introduced on the station you grew up listening to, it really is all the boxes ticked.

Today's *YouTube* or *Spotify* audience is slightly different, but before that kind of platform came along, every youngster in the world was either introduced to pop music by their parents or through the magic of radio. This was the dream come true.

Getting on TV was almost impossible. BBC shows didn't really want you so soon after *X Factor* and ITV understandably wanted to promote that year's cream of the crop, whom they would inevitably promote from the following October. If everybody who had been in our year suddenly started releasing before the winner then there was a danger of affecting the credibility of the act, and then surely, there was no point in winning the thing. This pattern had been set way back in 2005, when Brookstein released his album in the May of that year but G4, who came second, had already stolen a march with great success by the February – just three months after the show had concluded.

So, I continued to gig around the UK, but by late 2013, I knew that this particular phase of my life was over. Sam Bailey had made it as an Over. I was just another nearly man. I had a fanbase and had achieved more than I could have ever imagined, but I recognised that I had gone as far as I could.

It was time for Plan B.

Chapter Twenty-Four

I began 2014 fresh from *Peter Pan* the musical. I changed management – again. Finally, I decided to do something that I had always wanted to do. I launched my own academy. I know how beneficial it had been to sneak out behind my Dad's back to start learning my trade, *and* I recognised how different everything now was with social media, and the quickest route to stardom being reality TV. Just one individual through my doors might make it one day – but that wouldn't be the success story.

At the back of my mind were the thousands who were aspired to either start on that route and might get binned off along the way, or would never feel that ambition because they could not quite break out of their own mind, like I had struggled to do and would therefore live a lifetime of mental torment wondering what if.

I knew that I was in the right place to help these people who wanted it and I had experienced both scenarios. Deep down, whilst striving for excellence, I was clear that I also had the experience to help those who might struggle.

So, I set it up in Kirkdale, Liverpool, with three main coaches, specialising in singing, drama and dance. I wanted to fill a proper void from the ages of three to 19 that didn't really exist when I was growing up, and the timing felt right.

We launched in the June, with support from the Merseyside crème-de-la-crème! Cilla, Paul O'Grady, Jane McDonald and Gary Barlow all sent messages. Terri Dwyer, Tina Malone, Bruce Jones and Danniella Westbrook attended the launch.

I had got to know Dani in particular the previous Christmas when we were in *Sleeping Beauty* together at the King's Theatre in Southsea. I was pretty much a regular on the panto circuit by this time, mixing it with other people in my position who had experienced a moment of fame, and were good enough to continue to get regular work. Over the years, I ran into ex *Big Brother* contestants and actors from beloved shows like *Waterloo Road,* but it was Danniella who I really bonded with. You will have read a lot about her– most of it problematic – but this was a particularly low time for her.

We bonded instantly and she needed a shoulder to cry on. She was heading for divorce and had almost no support. The final straw had come when her husband had refused to come to see her. So, I invited her to move in with me in my apartment for the duration of the panto.

I got to know the real her. Like all friends, we had our ups and downs, falling out when we went on holiday together the following year. Generally, I would work in pantomime for the festive season and concentrate on the academy at the weekends throughout the year.

Within no time at all a certain show called, asking if we had anybody good at the academy? I later learned that the same had happened to Spike from the boyband 911, who was also doing a similar kind of thing in nurturing young talent.

Yep – the *X Factor* called a few times, but I politely declined, saying that my pupils were not ready yet. At that time, I don't think I had any intention of putting my pupils through something that had nearly broken me personally. I would feel completely responsible if I sent someone to the show who was not able to cope with it. However, if over the course of time some pupils did have the right combination of strength and talent, then that would be something to discuss with their parents later down the line, but not in our first couple of years.

Those first few hopefuls in my initial intake would have seen a different Christopher Maloney to the one they saw on television. The shivering wreck who they had all read about, who came so close and then disappeared into a meltdown, was now somebody else. In every sense of the word.

I clearly had not recovered fully from the breakdown, because it was the online trolling from years before that now led me to a course of action which was almost unstoppable to this day.

In 2013, I *had* finally made it onto *Loose Women* on ITV, and it was here where I became friends with Jane McDonald. She had also worked the cruise ships and stolen the nation's hearts in the show. Naturally, we shared that past but she was always sticking up for me when others piled in with the masses. In fact, she asked me to do a duet with her. In short, she knew exactly the journey I had been on. None of that mattered at this point. The fact is that I looked shocking on television.

I knew it too and couldn't stand it.

After we finished the show, I got a message from a company in Yorkshire, who specialised in hair transplant. That look in my one pop video had never left my thoughts. Frankly, it had been just the call I was waiting for.

Or, so I thought.

I went to see them and, before I knew it, I was under the knife for the first time. The surgeon stripped back my scalp from ear to ear and set to work on me. With no anaesthetic, it was the most painful thing that I have ever experienced.

I literally felt every crunch. I survived the ordeal only on my own Valium. Nine hours of pain, and the result? Elephant Man. My head swelled to balloon size. Stupidly, I had no way of getting home either, so I ordered a cab to Sheffield Station then took the train, all the time with a hat lightly pulled over my head.

I was in a state of shock. I needed thirty stitches.

My knowledge of plastic surgery to this point was confined to those big American stars, who appeared to be so fake that it was unreal, and a little bit of trout pout from certain rich and famous people. I didn't think for one moment it could go so horribly wrong like this.

I tried to hide it on the way back, but there was nowhere to go. Everybody was staring at me. Blood was squirting all over the place, with hairs shooting out from the incisions. I got off at Liverpool Lime Street matted in red. It looked like a murder scene.

When I got home, I remained bed-ridden for fourteen days. It was a nightmare, except for the fact that those bad dreams happen in your *sleep,* and this was playing out whilst I was wide awake. I *couldn't* get my head down and tossing and turning meant that the dissoluble stitches at the back had to be removed by my own doctor. I resorted to trying to kip in an upright position – almost impossible to do.

I was in agony and in a complete absence of aftercare. I am scarred for life from ear to ear.

The only way to attempt to survive this was to put my hand into my own pocket to repair this botch job, and that meant travelling to London to see another specialist surgeon. Only six months later did the healing begin.

I could never have imagined that anyone could become addicted to plastic surgery, but this is where the trail starts. You can see that initially, it was not chasing after the next perfect look or trying to create a new me. It was simply the desire to repair that hair which then made me think 'why not?' and from there an attempt to mend the mess led me to another clinic. After that, I was unstoppable.

It started with a genuine medical desire – not a necessity, just a wish to sort out that scalp, but the mess they made of it forced me to question everything and before long I was booking in for a nose job.

Guess what? I hated that too. I preferred my old honker! Again, I was left in so much pain and this time felt disgusted with *my*self. They had gone up through my right nostril leaving me struggling to breathe. I have no idea how they normally do these things but this felt terribly wrong to me – at least in the state I was left in.

I really did not know what to do and it started to dawn on me that some people undergoing treatment were doing so to mend previous efforts. Naturally, this is where the addiction lies, because there is a massive gulf between 'it's just not quite right' or 'perfect' which are probably the two likeliest after-thoughts. If it is just not quite right, or worse, you go again.

I returned to Sheffield, having called the original company in a rage. Perhaps fearing the negative publicity, having called me off the back of a TV show, they promised to make it all better.

So, they set about taking a strip out of my head bit by bit. Something went wrong again and I was back on the tablets, nearly hooked on Valium. My nose did at least start to settle.

Back I went to the surgeon. Once again, the results were worse.

At this point, I was in despair. Never mind that I looked like shit, I was in incredible pain. I really didn't know what to do because any attempt to make things better had just had the opposite effect.

In desperation, I tried the approach that had got me here in the first place. I took to television once more. Looking back, I don't really understand how it came to this: In 2012, I appear in one of the biggest shows on TV. I do the tour and leave the bad stuff behind. I get a deal and have reasonable success but yet by 2014 and 2015, I am making regular trips to plastic surgery clinics, including resorting to Poland. It became the theme of my life. It took over.

On 27 May 2015, I opened up to Philip Schofield and Christine Bleakley that it was the trolling during the show that helped bring me to this place. They placed a caption on the screen, announcing that I had spent £60,000 on surgery. Online bullies calling me Mr Potato Head meant that suddenly I was in Warsaw awaiting yet more surgery.

And the process was both draining and filled me with little confidence. On the first day I would just sleep. The next they would sort my hair, the third they would do my nose, followed by my eyelids and, at the end of the week, they would finish me off by giving me a new set of top teeth. I don't know what happens in Hollywood but I went for the lot – a total transformation. When I think back on it, it was a huge risk because all my previous experiences had literally left me scarred.

Five consecutive days under the knife both racked up the bills and left me shattered. If you have ever had any operation in hospital, and you can remember how knackered you were after, well I went a full week of surgery. I really was putting it all on the line. I placed my total faith in the clinic in Poland. To date, I had not one piece of plastic surgery that I thought was worth it or had improved me.

I can be a bit vain – I accept that – but it was the online trolling and my breakdown that had driven me to this, and now it was having a spiralling effect that was racing out of control, as I threw money at pain, in search of repairing the previous shoddy work. They really had won.

And when I woke up, praying that this time it would be better, I could not have been more devastated.

I panicked.

What the fuck had I done? One thing would catch my eye then, in the mirror, I would spot something else. I hated it and it looked agonizing. I had thrown the works at my new look and broke down in tears at the result. And this had to be the new me now. There was no turning back. Never mind getting a train home with blood flying everywhere, this was pretty much final. I couldn't get more work done to salvage this. I knew people would look me in the eye and think – well, frankly, it didn't even quite feel like my eye anymore!

I looked fake. It was all too plastic. But at the moment, I was swollen and out of shape. And I couldn't really see beyond that. The thought of ever doing anything in public again horrified me instantly. Just getting out of the clinic to the airport was already a step too far.

Mortified does not do it justice. On so many levels it hurt. I felt foolish. The look appalled me. I felt my credibility had also been destroyed. I looked like my ego had run away with me. And I was in agony. It was just a disaster.

It took at least a fortnight for the swelling to go down. That was the severity of the work. Then like a new day dawning, I suddenly realised it was all actually alright. They *had* done a good job after all. I went from one extreme to the other, suddenly falling in love with the new look. I realised that I had been tired after all the work and that obviously, you don't draw any conclusions until that swelling had subsided, but I had got myself into such an emotional state that I lost patience and could not see the bigger picture.

Now, finally, I was so happy that I decided to pretty much have surgery every year. They could tinker with me as much as they wanted. I was just so relieved that someone could do a good job and that actually they had made me look better that I thought, 'why not'. They *could* keep going and, as a result, I would return to Poland many times.

But it wasn't the vanity issue that kept me coming back. It was the victory. That I had beaten the trolls who had looked like they were going to strike me out twice – once with the online bullying and then with the surgery, which I felt forced to undertake and had failed so miserably first time around.

On one occasion, I was to go back and the consultant told me that what I was proposing would not look right. A friend had come with me too, and simply told me that I didn't need it and I would look worse. For once, I took their advice and got the next plane home.

But the fact remained, I was now addicted to surgery.

That meant that by the time the public saw me next, I was not the same Christopher Maloney they had last seen. And when they did set eyes on me, they were about to get an overdose. I had signed up to do *Celebrity Big Brother 2016.*

The show was to air in the January. In the previous August, *Channel 5* had been in touch to sound me out. There are really only two reasons for doing a show like this, and you know what they are – career management and the cash.

I had read so many times about the vast amounts of money on offer, and of course was not daft enough to think that the sums were all real, but I did realise that if I went in the house I would have a chance for people to see the real me, whilst picking up some potentially easy money.

Plus – I had seen the show regularly from 2000 and, just like the *X Factor,* it was an incredible feeling to think that you could suddenly go from watching your favourite show to being part of it. I did laugh to myself that, whilst I might genuinely be surrounded by celebrities, I realised that I had that tag too, albeit in a lesser way.

Anyway, when they put the cash on the table, I surprised myself by initially saying no. I remembered that I had always told my friends that I would never do a show like this, despite loving to watch it. I think I was sticking to my principles that I just wanted to sing, which was really cutting off my new nose to spite my new face, considering I had already done that on one show and had done as well as I could. Nor did anybody want to see me do that again.

While the channel went away to think about it, I did too, and talked myself round. They did come back with a better offer, but the money had not been the issue. Easy to say, I know. I just concluded that even though it could be seen all live but still went out as an edited show, which in the past it had been accused of manipulating what they aired, I hoped that it would be a different kind of Director's Cut.

Equally, whilst the trolls might be out in force, because shows like this went hand in hand with their social media audience, they wouldn't get to me directly, because I couldn't see it in real time. There, in a nutshell were the two differences – the edit would hopefully be more sympathetic and the keyboard warriors would only be arguing with themselves.

There was also going to be a psychologist on standby, which gave me additional comfort. This had always been part of the show's armoury. I was just never clear from watching the show whether it was part of the entertainment or a very real duty of care, but the network bosses were very good to me in all the pre-amble and assured me that it was genuine.

Something else was fundamental in my thinking. That diva word. I had never been able to shake that off, and even though it had been four years since *X Factor,* it was just one of the phrases that came up if you googled me, so I couldn't put to bed all those nasty comments from the past, where I was supposed to have made excessive demands. I think the diva word might have been the reason the network went for me. Diva to them might equate to entertainment and viewing figures. I don't know, but for me it could mean quashing the diva label once and for all.

I *was* worried going in whether *Channel 5* might stitch me up in some way, but I guess everybody is, and my own paranoia probably played a big part. I just figured that even if they manipulated the edit in some way, if I only gave them the real me then the truth would shine through.

There was only one thing left to consider. Who were my housemates? Inevitably, as the launch approached, all sorts of names were being banded about. Some of them, I had to google. All I knew was that I was going in and so could anybody else. I had no prior knowledge of the other contestants. In fact, I went into hiding a couple of days before the show began, just to keep a lid on everything from my end!

I kept telling myself that there was nothing to lose and that it was a great opportunity, but the fact of the matter is that I was shitting it. That launch day gives you a lot of time to think. I cannot tell you how many times in your head you think you will do this to the audience or that to the camera or practise a funny ad-lib to the host, Emma Willis. Nervous energy persuades you that one minute you have a bright idea of how to make an entrance. But you have all day to change your mind and talk yourself out of it. It is impossible to concentrate. You don't really participate in any of the conversations around you with any sincerity. You are only half-listening. You just keep fretting about how it is going to come across and then you worry about all the stupid things, like no mobile for however long, no Gary, the press, Nan, trolls – you know they can't get to you when you are in there, but they are already getting to you anyway, because you know what is coming…all

149

that stuff. And that is before potentially falling foul of a housemate or an unfavourable edit.

Then suddenly it all starts. The choreography is under way. You immediately remind yourself that it is not about you. They are making a TV show and so I don't even remember if I was third or fourth going in. Suddenly, a runner taps on the door and the car starts, and the next thing you are in the slot the producers have allocated you, within a narrow window of time, and you are on the stage with a screaming audience all around you and videos playing on the screen. At that moment, all the thinking and planning that you have had time to do all day evaporates. Because you are suddenly *in* the moment. It begins. It has begun. You are back on the telly – and it is live – for as long as it lasts.

One thing I do remember is that I enter to booing. I didn't take it too seriously. It was more pantomime than anything malicious, and even if it was based on a previous pre-conception, it was very much in one ear and out the other. Plus, I had just come from playing Captain Hook in *Peter Pan,* so maybe I was just used to it from that. The travelling sound leaves you so quickly. Before you know it there is much more to contend with. Make no doubt though, I am terrified.

Of course, once you go through those doors, your brain splits as dramatically as if the plastic surgeon in Sheffield had been cutting it open. You know you are live on TV (even though it is probably the last time you think about it), but you are also meeting the housemates and know that there is some embarrassment ahead, as the pecking order begins to emerge as to levels of fame, which ones you know, and if they recognise *you*. The truth is, as we all know, that once you enter at launch, the camera is on the outside of the house and the action is all about the next person to go in, so even though you feel that pressure of the spotlight, it is a wasted emotion. The public are watching something else. Others may have felt differently. There are always a few people who think that the sun revolves around them. I figure that there will be two pecking orders – the first will be the way each contestant sees themselves in relation to everyone else. The second comes after a little delay – when the public starts ranking them. I recall in 2006 when they threw a complete unknown into the house by the name of Chantelle Houghton, and the idea was that she would feign a showbiz past, which they fell for to the degree that she became famous in her own right through the show, indeed winning it and by marrying one of the other contestants, Preston. That year, as a joke to the viewer, they were asked to rank the contestants early on, as to who was the most and least famous. It stuck with me and the fact that she won the whole thing, I guess clarified my theory of two pecking orders. I knew that once I was in there I would be myself, let everyone see the real me and the world of pre-conception would look a different place whenever I came out.

In fact, you really didn't have to win it. Look at all those times where the runner-up had done so much better than the winner. It all seemed to matter so much at the time, but after a while, nobody remembered or cared. There were – I concluded – only two likely outcomes in the long term. Would you be remembered for one particular incident and could you survive the edit, so the public almost didn't recognise you from whom they believed you were.

Obviously, I had a new face too!

My partner, Gary, once joked to me, 'When you go in *Celebrity Big Brother,* I will know you are a celeb then.'

The only thing is – he hadn't seen the line up!

One by one they all came in. Where do we begin? I am standing next to Kim Kardashian's best mate, Jonathan Cheban.

Then there is *Hollyoaks* cast member, Stephanie Davis – supposedly fired from the show, accused of lateness and unprofessionalism. I had seen her on a few nights out around Liverpool.

Next, oh my goodness, Gemma Collins. She had done three days in *I'm a Celebrity* and countless series of *The Only Way Is Essex* (TOWIE). She really was full time reality.

Then comes Scotty T – from *Geordie Shore,* followed by Kristina Rihanoff, one of the professional dancers on *Strictly Come Dancing.* Megan from *Ex on the Beach* … Jeremy McConnell, a former Mr Ireland contestant…Tiffany Pollard, an American reality show queen…

David Gest, friend of *The Jacksons*… ex-boxer Winston McKenzie, singer and actor Darren Day, *EastEnders* legend and star of stage and screen, John Partridge, Nancy Dell'Olio, the former partner of Sven, the one-time England football manager, Angie Bowie, and finally – well would you believe it? – Danniella Westbrook, whom I have barely seen we had had our little disagreement, is in the house. I must admit that I didn't recognise a few of my fellow housemates initially. Darren – I recognised from *Joseph,* which I loved. I had met David once at a party. Tiffany struck me as having anger issues, and I had actually seen some of her shows. I knew Kristina by name, adored John from his work, loved the Kardashians, wasn't really enamoured with Gemma, and Nancy amused me because she claimed to have Champagne listed on her rider and, as VIP demands go, that was a proper celebrity.

Within moments, I have forgotten the cameras are there. That remained the case until I exited three weeks or so later.

The 'fun and games' start immediately. My suitcase is confiscated straightaway. I think it is a task. They can't really have claimed to have lost it. They are not, after all, an airline. They are just moving it from outside the set to in it. The result is that I have to wear the same clothes for the first three days.

I begin to stink instantly. I realise it is part of a team game, not designed to place me as a victim, unless they are hoping I have a diva strop, but more to see how others react to me. John Partridge is the first to come good, offering to share his clothes with me. Nobody else offers help. I am without product too so, as you can imagine, this is heart-breaking! I spend all that money getting my face and hair sorted in Poland, and then I can't get my face and hair sorted.

I decide to sleep in my clothes. It gets better. I am sharing a bed with Danniella. It seems a petty thing now to have previously fallen out, given that we were good friends. Equally, I think it would be really bad form to not be allies in the house. I didn't really want to air stuff like that in front of the cameras, so that means just bonding slowly.

The first sleep and how you wake up from it is often a measurement of how you feel about the house. The glitz and giddiness of launch have long passed. You often talk deep into that first morning. Then, I am sure, you wake to think 'what have I done?'

For me, that meant instant claustrophobia. I had lost track of time almost immediately and that didn't help. At night, the shutters went down. In the morning, they go up. They are your only markers as to where you are in the day, and I am the kind of person who needs to know what time it is. It panics me otherwise. Even though at night, you were aware of almost eerie ghost-like figures and producers whispering, passing notes and scuttling behind the scenes, they are isolated moments. You are not on a TV set. You are in a house. It is, I guess, more like imprisonment.

On the second day – even though I am already in the task of being deprived of my clothes – the actual tasks begin. Many of these seem terribly contrived but you have to go along of course. It's all part of the show. We *can't* just sit there all day, even though there is a lot of that. The tasks are clearly designed to cause controversy, separate and divide and, whilst winning them can provide treats or immunity from eviction, they are for entertainment purposes. I know that the public will be noting who is a team player, who moaned, and who didn't help. By 2016, you'd think most people had an awareness of how shows like this work. Although, I imagine that others, like Angie Bowie maybe weren't quite as aware. I am not sure whether Nancy had ever watched it. It is very easy to forget when you are on a task the reasons you are being asked to do them. At least half the house seemed to come from some sort of reality TV that you would think they would be wise to the

153

whole process. As time unfolded, there was almost no evidence of that.

Chapter Twenty-Five

In many of the tasks, it seemed there were echoes of previous years or some that I thought were identical. I guess, if you watch shows like *Strictly* or *I'm A Celebrity* they seem to stick to a standard format every series. But, it's the individuals and the chemistry that makes them different each year, with the public picking their favourites each week.

So, when we woke up to find that we were being asked to rank ourselves from most to least annoying, to me, it had echoes of that Preston-Chantelle year – which I think is actually a very good, divisive task. The viewer has their own opinion (and inevitably there are a few that you might not have never heard of) and the house instantly creates a pecking order that leaves everybody looking over their shoulder.

So, voting on least/most annoying was not quite as dramatic as playing the fame game, but there were similarities, of course. You were being asked to decide, based on one night in the house.

Jeremy, Scotty T and Stephanie *won* the vote in that they were the most annoying, which I was surprised at. The prize for this task was to 'unlock the rest of the house' and get Danniella, Darren and John 'out of the box'.

There were 1500 keys to choose from. I always felt that was a miscount and there had in fact been 1501, as it seemed that someone had already thrown Gemma's away.

In no time at all, Gemma was threatening to leave – part-real and part-drama, I suspect. She must have kicked down the door three or four times, only to be escorted back in by security.

Some of the tasks really felt quite dull at the time, especially when you just read them back now. They all had a purpose though. Hot on the heels of annoying and lockout was a simple split the house into two scenario. Each team's Captain would read out a series of facts. Then you had to decide which housemate from the opposite side matched the fact. It told you a little about a few individuals, gave you a conversation starter, but most importantly, you always knew these bits were going to make the edit, and you could end up automatically facing the public vote for eviction.

So, something clearly so simple and seemingly meaningless had massive overtones. The house began to divide. But I can't imagine it making interesting television. One task involved sitting on some sort of mushroom contraption – just rooted on your arse with a toadstool up your backside. The only problem was that the kit broke, sending a nail right into my head, causing me to nearly lose my eye. I was taken away for emergency repairs – the doctor fixing me up with butterfly stitches.

Some stuff did *not* make the edit when actually it would have made extraordinary viewing. The magic mushrooms were not the only time the paramedics were called.

Once when we were all eating, Scotty T started moving his hands about all agitated. The next thing he was turning purple and blue. A piece of meat was lodged in his throat and he was literally choking to death. But most of us thought he was messing about. John, again, was the first to spot when a housemate needed help and saved his life with the Heimlich manoeuvre. The meat went flying and Scotty hit the deck. This was not shown.

There was plenty more to come. Maybe there were some things that I didn't see at the time, or have come to understand since, but it felt like there was some unsavoury stuff going on.

Tiffany had smuggled in Valium. Stephanie had some fun with Jeremy under the covers. The claim that she had been sacked from *Hollyoaks* because of her behaviour proved true, even though she is one of my best friends now. The notion that she entered the show to turn things around soon went out the window. We *did* have lots of chats, but this was the wrong place for her. Relationships that have formed over the years on reality shows often bear no semblance to reality when it is over. Steph went on to have a baby with Jeremy, but was badly

156

beaten in an assault. When things were really bad after the show, I took her out shopping and then back for drinks at mine. Jeremy called and ordered her to get out of my house there and then. She upped and left in an instant, leaving her bags behind. It was sorrowful to watch.

He later was sent to prison.

It is extraordinary to think how he seemed to pull the wool over people's eyes. He had seemed lovely inside the house. Watching that year, you would never know what was to come. The whole fooling around together on set felt extremely wrong to me. Everyone was shouting at them to get a room. They had one indeed. They just shared it with the rest of us.

I think that when two people become an item in the house, it can't really do them any favours. It might get them a magazine deal after, but it creates two distinct possibilities, whether the 'romance' lasts the duration of the show, or if it is a moment of madness. That stain lingers and creates an island. It would have been the last thing on my mind – as gorgeous as John Partridge is!

For me, to throw yourself at the task, have fun, and correct people's impression, was the reason I was there and in a beautiful moment, David was asked to organise a talent show.

His whole life had been about working the best in the music business, re-uniting *The Jacksons* and promoting some of America's biggest acts, but now he was choreographing some camp bloke from Liverpool who had come third in a UK talent show. But I loved it.

Jonathon, Nancy and Tiffany were the judges; Angie became Dermot! Stephanie was James Arthur – only in the sense that she won!

It was an incredible sensation to parody the *X Factor*, knowing that it didn't matter one jot and, if anything, my credibility might rise because of it. It made me laugh, but it meant a lot when John, who had been a very credible reality judge on a BBC1 show, said I had been robbed in 2012. Honestly, there could not have been two better candidates to seal the night in a dance-off than him and I. I loved dressing up as Cheryl Cole to really emphasise the send up. Plus, of course, that was something that I only normally did for Gary at weekends and Bank holidays!

Some tasks bored the hell out of me, like the Puppets and the Puppeteers. The former was answerable to the latter in a master-servant relationship. Puppets could only eat food provided to them; their beds were replaced with boxes. Unbelievably, that meant that Gemma was now my boss and my, did she seem to revel in it. I guess I'm considered an easy target. To me, this task seemed like a horrible opportunity to bully someone.

I was now living off crackers and spam and lasted four days before vomiting everywhere on a fermented egg. It had stretched my patience in the house. It was a sort of pivotal moment that broke my spirit as the trolls had done in *X Factor*. And at the end of it all, we failed the task.

To me, it certainly seemed to suit her calling the shots. Everyone was in this show for their own reasons, I guess, but I don't know what hers were. For the most part, she didn't seem interested in participating in the tasks. When the housemates were called outside for a 6 am spin class, she just stayed in bed, announcing to Big Brother that 'I'm not getting up. I'm not performing today.'

I didn't understand why someone would behave like that, having agreed to come on the show.

On another occasion, though, when I decided to cook everyone a hearty meal, she suddenly declared that she would help me. She started cutting up the onions, but tragically nearly cut her thumb off. Hospital beckoned – stitches required.

As I recall the tasks now, it does not take away from the fact that 99% of the time I *was* actually a bit bored. We *did* just sit around a lot. You realise now how important those luxury items are that you are allowed to bring in. The only problem was that mine were my fags and they had disappeared out of my drawer. There were moments of real fun too, though. Darren had brought in two bottles of spray tan – one light and one dark. Being imprisoned drives you to crazy extremes. That will explain how I ended up with a light and dark tan on both sides of my face!

On Day Thirteen, Tiffany's task was to spread rumours about the housemates. I think that there was more than one candidate for that task. It could have been seen as an underhanded move or playing to some of the contestants' strengths, depending on your viewpoint. There were lip-synch competitions and dancing routines too. In my view, I guess it was all fairly superficial, apart from the undertones, of course.

But, after the accidents, strangely, this dicing with death thing would not go away. We couldn't possibly know it at the time, but we had no idea what was to come or how bad things would get.

Chapter Twenty-Six

David was dead. They both were.

'Day Seven in the *Big Brother* house. Angie and Tiffany are in the kitchen.'

Angie Bowie made Tiffany promise that she would not say a word to anybody. Then she delivered the crushing blow.

'David's dead.'

Tiffany began to wail hysterically, grabbing Angie, pleading with her to see if she was serious. Darren was outside with myself and a couple of others smoking. We heard the cries from there.

Tiffany told Angie she thought she was joking.

'It just happened now,' Angie told her. 'Cancer, and you gotta stay quiet.'

Tiffany was hysterical, crying her eyes out, saying she needed a drink. We decided to go back in and Tiffany announced that she couldn't keep it a secret as she fell into Angie's arms.

'I'm not able to say anything,' she cried. 'She told me that David is dead.'

'No,' I screamed.

Then everybody knew.

Danniella told Tiff to go and talk to the Diary Room. I'm not sure that was the best advice at the time.

Angie just kept repeating that she had fucked up.

Darren and I did the obvious thing. We went to David's bed and pulled back the cover. Through all the commotion there was a still corpse lying there. But it was very much alive. David was not dead.

That sent Tiffany into a further extreme. She was now beyond hysterical and fearing betrayal as a result of a sick joke.

'Why the fuck would she do that to me?' she pleaded.

'Keep them apart,' someone shouted as though it was going to come to blows.

'What did I do?' asked Angie.

'You told her David was dead with cancer,' Danniella said.

'Yes, he is,' she replied.

'He is in there asleep,' she answered.

It was a classic piece of tragic comedy. Watching it back and knowing the truth makes you feel immense guilt, but I am afraid it is one of those awful uncomfortable moments where everybody got the wrong end of the stick and viewers must have squirmed at the car-crash TV.

But he wasn't.

Then Angie cleared the matter up:

'David, my ex-husband,' she announced.

There was about a second's silence, before Danniella announced that she was off to calm it down.

But curiously, nobody said:

'What, David Bowie is dead?'

Whatever your taste in music, but surely hadn't everybody on the planet heard of him?

What we didn't know at the time, of course, was that 2016 turned out to be a year when so many big stars would pass away, from Prince to George Michael. Quite a few went in that January when *Big Brother* was on. Nobody even knew David Bowie was poorly.

Angie took to the Diary Room and announced 'It's a mess.'

'Take a moment, Angie,' the faceless voice responded.

Outside, Tiffany could not be calmed down, clearly having misheard that when she asked Angie, 'David Gest', Angie had only heard it as 'David's dead.'

Everyone was confused and Danniella added:

'David Bowie ain't dead either.'

But he was.

John came out from the shower in just his towels to set the record straight.

David was dead. But David wasn't.

Angie had talked about David a lot. David was shocked and didn't have a clue what was going on. Are you following me?

David *was* dead but *David* wasn't a well man at the time either, but we just couldn't really see it in the house. Worryingly, nor could anybody outside of the house. I had heard all this stuff over the years about psychometric tests on contestants, but nobody had realised that David wasn't fit to be in there.

Someone asked Angie to tell us more about her David, but, in her state, she just told us to read her 'fucking book'.

Many of us were becoming friends, but now, tragedy had ripped the house apart. I wasn't in it to win it. I just wanted to stay as long as I could to change perceptions. This overshadowed everything. We all had numerous opportunities to walk, but this really was a cloud that would hang over the house. One couple were sleeping together that would ultimately end in disastrous consequences. There had been numerous injuries. And now David was dead. But he wasn't. Not yet anyway.

Chapter Twenty-Seven

I had decided to speak to the psychologist. There was a sense of collectiveness in what happened but it also seemed to split ranks. The death of anyone outside the house was more important than a TV show. But David Bowie was obviously huge news.

I began to wonder what else was going on. How was this being written up? I even wondered whether the show would continue, given this new development. But, of course, it did. I think it left people feeling helpless, I know I did. There was a lot of time to be alone with your thoughts.

So, I went to the Diary Room.

It is a curious mixture of realities. You do forget that you are on a TV show, but also when something like this happens it jolts you right back and you remember that it is *only* just that. I asked the life coach if everything was alright. I had for the first time began to worry about how I was coming across, but it was moments like this that sparked that self-doubt.

'The Royal Family have all been shot. There are bugs all over the UK. Everyone's dead. There's no-one left on the outside,' was the answer.

'You're joking?' I asked.

Really, could I have been that detached from reality on a reality TV show that I believed him for a split second. Another example of how detached from reality you feel.

'Course, I'm joking,' he replied.

I was putting trust in the show, but I had suddenly panicked or become self-aware and started to worry about the impact on *my* family when I learned about David Bowie.

'Just continue to be yourself,' I was told.

That was probably the limit of what they were allowed to say, walking that fine line between mental health support for the individual and the good of the overall show.

At that point, I read clues into his words. I decided that I was doing fine and there had been no backlash against me. In fact, I found out afterwards that there was no negative press about me whilst I was in the house.

The effect of David Bowie's death and David Gest's survival was that I really started to dream badly. There was too much time to think and I began to have recurring dreams. Granddad featured a lot and so did other dead relatives, just clapping their hands at me night after night.

I was not sure what it meant, other than the tone of the house had changed on David's death. I would wake every morning, trying to convince myself that I hadn't had the dream, when I had, but I felt it was a sign that I was getting ready to leave.

It all changed with David. It didn't feel right any more. My mind was affected by it and I didn't really want to stay. I had made my point too, that people could see the real me and I knew the end was coming.

When the night arrived that it was time to go, I think you can see it in my face. I know. John puts my coat on, and later told me that he was really sad to see me leave. You literally have five seconds to get out of the house. I am not sure what really happens if you linger for six, but that was the drill.

I remembered the jeers I received when I went in. It felt a lifetime ago. The reality was that it was twenty-something days. To see daylight was extraordinary. To be met by family was incredible. I really didn't give a shit about anything else.

But I did notice one thing. There were no boos this time. I left to cheers. I soon learned that that no other housemate had actually nominated me. I was stunned, relieved and somehow felt my faith in human nature had been restored, but actually that is a comment which is a bit lost in showbiz, because it wasn't real and it didn't matter.

Week after week I *won* the *X Factor* on the public vote. Yet, I felt the need to go in the house so that same public could see me for real – who I actually was. And they had voted pretty much the same – except they had had to vote *for* me this time, bar the one occasion I had missed amnesty from eviction.

The public were constant. The voters were consistent. But in the bubble, my head had been mashed with trolls, PR machines, second-guessing and the mouths of rivals. But the audience never wavered and in the pressure cooker of this show, other housemates found me just normal.

Face to face nominations had been a nightmare – a real test of nerve and character. I threw up after nominating Tiffany. But generally, I don't think I had been two faced at all – as is the way with shows like this and despite me obviously being on my second face!

It is safe to say in fact that the crowd went mental when I exited. I had no idea what to expect and I was stunned by the reaction. I *didn't* get lost in the moment this time. I made a considered split-second decision to lap this up. I had no idea why they were so supportive and favourable, and I knew I would find out soon, but I just went with it and took it as a nod that I had done OK. I decided, after 22 days, to just milk it.

When Emma Willis came over to me on the stage, it really was on a par with standing on the X on the *X Factor* stage. Actually, of course, *Big Brother* had been on our screens longer, but, to me, sometimes *Channel 4* or *5* shows didn't seem to quite have the lasting impact. My interview with Emma was pretty cut and dry. It was the standard pleasantries before they cut to an ad-break, but then you go onto a full-on one to one chat on *Big Brother's Little Bit On The Side,* in which you really open up, free from what seems like a panto audience outside. You do feel like you have gone from a live TV show to a sofa chat with a few mates, when the reality is that you are *more* on TV on the spin-off show than at the live eviction.

Of course, they asked me about Gemma. In fact, it felt like that was all they really asked me about. I didn't hold back. I ripped into her. In my mind, the time she frogmarched me to the toilets to abuse me, knowing that the cameras were not on in there, even though the microphones were, came immediately to mind. It was as if she knew exactly what she was doing, as though she had actually done her research before she came in. I was not playing her game – or any game – and free from the confines of the *actual* show or the edit, I told them so. I hated that woman.

And I did.

As I walked away into the sunset I felt it was job done. I also had the sense to realise that the old adage 'today's news, tomorrow's chips' applied to this show maybe even more than any other – the *Daily Star* was intravenously dripped to the show, but almost with no lasting impact. I had survived diva and other slurs.

All I knew was that I had been well paid and well received, and in the world of reality TV if you can move the circus on a little and people can see you in the context of another outlet, with different principles then, in today's age, many people often only remembered you for the last thing they saw you in.

To that note, the balance was re-addressed. I was content with my lot. 2016 had started well but I had no idea what was next. My fifteen minutes of fame were more than likely running out.

Chapter Twenty-Eight

David *was* dead.

David was dead and David is dead. David and David were dead. They are both dead. In less than three months after coming out of the *Big Brother* house, in which he really did not appear well, or any shade of the character he had portrayed over the years, the Gest machine seemed to have run out of gas.

Anybody who has lost somebody will always take as a reference the last time that you spoke. I spoke with David just the day before. He was always so full-on and even then, with just 24 hours left to live, his whole life was a performance. I don't know if it shielded a lonely, depressed man, whose limelight papered over the cracks. Some might have said that he was passed his best, professionally. For some, people, after all, do not go on shows like *Celebrity Big Brother* when they are flying. He had chosen to settle in England, when outside of *I'm A Celebrity* he wasn't so well known here. And just three months before in the house, I could tell he wasn't good.

It must have taken so much effort generally being David Gest, but when your body is about to reject you for the final time, it was surely beyond exhausting. Obviously when he called me for the last time, I had no idea that time had caught up with him. I couldn't see him on the call, but it was the usual David.

'Christopher, every time I call you, you don't answer my calls,' he had begun.

Then two hours later we finished chatting.

And it was true, I had been neglectful. I wonder too just how many times he had rung someone, looking for a friend and they had not picked up either. His life had been about networking to do the deal. Now, I look back and sense that at the end of his, he wondered where all those people had gone.

I can imagine that in his prime, managing legendary American acts back home, he probably did his fair share of hanging up on people to play hardball. Now, his professional energy prolonged every call when I think it was companionship he craved. He was always telling me about some show he was planning and what we were going to do together. David was a dead man if he didn't have an idea to hatch, but now the lights had gone out for the final time.

I had hundreds of texts and voicemails from him, and even though I couldn't have done anything to prevent his death, I feel terrible that I had avoided his calls at times. You just needed a lot of time and a clear head to take the full-on David experience. I am not speaking ill of him. That is just who he was. Larger than life.

I liked him a lot. I saw a talented man, an incredible networker, with mind-blowing stories and connections. He made you believe that anything could happen, but it felt like he was in decline when we met, but did not change the fact that I bonded with him very quickly. I loved the guy. Whether out of insecurity, insincerity, or incredible altruism, he gave and you wanted to be part of it, and then you could bathe in his sunshine too.

He was found dead at The Four Seasons Hotel on 12 April, 2016 at London's Canary Wharf – so many miles from home, so lost and so lonely. Equally, so soon after being so public – almost less than three months after *Big Brother.*

He was 62, for Heaven's Sake, and passed away of a stroke. That was the official word. It is always tough when somebody you know dies, but when you have been with them ten weeks previously and their age is just so young, and you know that they did not look great, it is only hindsight that tells you how bad they obviously were.

I spent time with both the medics and psychologist in *Big Brother,* and I realise now that my angst and nervousness were nothing compared to him counting down to his final days. I recognise that anxiety is a real issue because I suffer from it, but having seen David have his last public moment so ill and so close to death put everything into context. You can learn to cope with such feelings of borderline depression – I think – if you can put things into perspective, and David's death gave me that.

After that last conversation, something had been bugging me. I didn't know he was going to die, of course, but I *had* not answered on so many occasions that I questioned why I had answered to speak to him that time, for what was to be the last time. On some subconscious level, I don't think I was surprised when his business manager called to tell me the worst.

I found myself saying all the usual stuff.

'It can't be true. We only spoke yesterday.'

But once it sunk in, I realised that it was most definitely was real. He hadn't looked well. I am grateful for that last conversation. He was upbeat to the last. Watching the story break on the TV news was beyond surreal. When you find yourself watching something where you know the people in question, you just sit there, mute, thinking that none of it is actually happening. You watch somebody you lived with being discussed by people who didn't know him at all, speculating and second-guessing, 'looking to bring you more on this story as it develops', when there was no more to bring you. David was dead.

That just left the funeral to contend with. I went with John Partridge and Danniella. We thought it was important that the house was represented. It really had been his last hurrah. The actress and singer, Kym Marsh, gave a very tearful reading, but the sad thing is that, for all the people he knew and had helped, there were no video messages from home. He had no family in attendance.

There was a party afterwards, but frankly, the day had been draining and everyone was tired and emotional. As people often say, he was taken too soon.

It is easy to say he was my friend. David was everybody's friend. You could see through all the bullshit and marvel at his connections – he could convince you that you would be doing a duet with any one of *The Jacksons* at any time – but he was actually genuine in his insincerity. He had

171

belief and made you believe. His product was invisible and I could see right through it too. He was *The Emperor's New Clothes* – showing no product of any substance, but still being able to believe in it and sell it, if that makes sense. He was a conjuror. A loveable rogue. A magician. A man with no real goods but the ability to flog the backside off them. In the time I knew him briefly, I knew him well. And I loved him dearly.

Chapter Twenty-Nine

Some people come out of these shows and suddenly find that there is some sort of deal on the table. I'd guess, most do not. I suspect that everyone walks in thinking it can be a game-changer. Occasionally you might get offered something really weird.

One of the main reasons for going into the house was the money, for Heaven's Sake. I sort of thought that to take the fee, keep your profile high and restore your reputation was enough.

So, when I was offered a record deal off the back of it, I instantly turned it down. That in itself is extraordinary on two fronts. If you think how people in the Overs category of the *X Factor* are often seen on screen saying that it 'really is their last chance', there is a sense of desperation that they will do almost anything – at that stage of life – to make that deal work. I had now, surprisingly, knocked it back.

But also, I am proud of the fact that I said no because it showed that I wasn't just going to accept *anything,* and that I had moved on from the dream of the *X Factor.* I had a sense of measurement and perspective. It was no longer the be-all and end-all. I had perspective – which I was really glad about. I had been there and done that. It didn't mean the world to me, as I had probably said in a million VTs, it wasn't my last chance, and I was not about to conform.

Most importantly, I wasn't bitter or regretful about *X Factor.* Any lingering ill-will over my struggling to cope had dissipated. There were now no consequences to live with. I guess, some people never got the answers they searched for from shows like these. I had suddenly realised that somehow, I'd worked it out for myself.

On the table now was a chance to do a swing album with the mighty *Universal* label. It would have been very easy to say yes – ridiculously so, and I could have played along, with the hope that it would lead to even bigger and better things. There was a theory in shows like *X Factor,* that if you towed the line for the first cover album then you might get to make the record that you really wanted second time around. It wasn't for me. I didn't fancy it. I certainly didn't need it. And I really didn't think it was going to do me any good. If anything, despite the fact that it was on a plate for me, I really didn't think it would do anything but backfire.

So, with that rejected, I had to find a new way.

So many people seemed to jump from one show to another, presumably for the fee. But few did with distinction. One person who did was Jake Quickenden, who appeared in my *X Factor* series (2012) *and* then again in 2016 and without having stormed either, surprisingly walked straight into *I'm A Celebrity* in the same year, possibly days after, and went on to finish second. Then, he won *Dancing On Ice* in 2018! That is the former lifeguard from Scunthorpe – a king of the celebrity shows, without technically being one in his own right. But then being one.

Fair play to him. I didn't really want that. It would be easy to take twice the national average salary or so and then cash in on the tour – a very obvious thing to do – but at some point you had to grow up and take the next step and that, ultimately, when the fifteen minutes of fame rolled into sixteen, meant doing something completely different.

The real key and strategy were to work out what you now knew about the media, production, and the shows people were likely to make, and why.

In August 2016, that is exactly what happened. Would I like to take part in a show called *Celebrity Trolls, We're Coming To Get You?*

Wow – that was one hell of an offer. I think it is fair to say that in titles like this most people have historically thought that celebrities – whether Y list or A list – had a huge element of 'they had it coming to them' and 'they got what they deserved'. The classic argument has always been that they courted publicity, so if they can't take it, don't dish it out.

All of which is true. Except it isn't. David's dead, but

he's not! Let's break this down:

In what way does someone who wants desperately, and is good enough to play football for a living, deserve personal grief? People sometimes argue that the Beckhams courted and used publicity to their own ends, so therefore they must take the rough with the smooth. I understand that, but if you strip it right back – a lad from Essex kicks a ball well, and marries a pop star.

Somehow, to some people, this gets translated into getting what you deserved. Everybody has shit days at the office. I'm sure Beckham had a few and many memorable ones. But as the saying goes, the mob are fickle. The social media crowd are exactly that, and also seem agitated by so many other factors, from what is going on in their own personal life, to the baiting of other trolls and the reaction they get from it. I think time is already showing that most trolls are revealing more about themselves in their actions than bringing down the subject of their abuse, even if in the first few years of social media they seemed to be getting away with it.

The keyboard warrior was now very much something we were accustomed to. The ability to hide in public, whilst attacking public figures was racing away from us at speed, and the legislation was not even crawling to catch up. It moved at a snail's pace. This was definitely one area where television could really move this problem along at pace.

I think also the notion that the 'celebrity' could or more importantly *would* fight back was new territory. You were expected to take it. It was part of the deal. But should it be? And was there a threshold of celebrity that also made it acceptable? If you were someone who had always been in the public eye, did that make you fair game, but if you were essentially a 'normal' person who had wandered into a talent contest and out again, was that different?

Had Jake, for example, absolutely chased fame and therefore deserved any grief over it – or was he just a human being riding his luck and now choosing that as the easiest way to make a living? Clearly, he was likely to say 'yes' to those

175

shows which, after *X Factor* were based on the notion of fame, but appearing fame-hungry or *just* taking the next job in a short-lived career were open to your own personal opinion. On the other hand, if you led a modest life, where you did not laud it in public, surely that meant you did not have to endure the wrath of the troll?

For me, the consequences had been dire. They took me to a breakdown during the *X Factor,* led to warnings that I would be shot during the tour, and had, at the very least, contributed to the whole plastic surgery journey – the result of which, back then was hiring surgeons to combat the paranoia created by the trolls.

Celebrities do google themselves. They like to see if they are trending or what other people are saying. I can tell you that none of them hear the good stuff – whatever the wealth. The small percentage of negativity always overrides the stuff you would print off and frame!

But it wasn't just those in the public eye. Take my good friend, Denise Fergus – mother of the murdered toddler, Jamie Bulger – a normal person, who did not crave any limelight, but found herself facing it head on. Social media gave everyone a voice, even the village idiot. In what way is that fair that these people can suddenly have their grief added to by nothing more than a username craving attention anonymously to an unlimited audience?

I think that is the point. The anonymity is the killer. Everybody at school witnesses some sort of bullying, whether they are the victim or not. Teachers used to say 'sticks and stones will break my bones, but names will never hurt'.

At the time, if you are on the receiving end, that does not help one bit. Years later, you reflect that the bully was often the one with the issues. But at least you could see them and you knew who they were. This was totally different. People were hiding in broad daylight and whilst some were kids, or homophobic Nazis in the making, others weren't. Some *were* respectable individuals, who often concealed the truth from the people they loved and lived with.

176

And that is exactly what we had here.

I was trolled by many people, but one in particular was in my sights – and I was not alone. Frankie Bridge from *The Saturdays* was fronting the show, amid a groundswell from celebrities wanting to re-address the balance. Nicola Mclean, Rebekah Vardy, Rebecca Adlington, Chloe Jasmin, and Sam Bailey were all to feature. This line up included an absolute legend who swam for her country and won Gold at The Olympics. Yet, people had found a reason to have a pop at her. I remember that some people would think her nose was fair game, but she probably had more talent in that part of her body than all the people who abused her put together – the nostrils obviously a key part of breathing when swimming, so what some ridiculed must have actually been a positive anyway. Clearly, in that list of names, there are a couple of people who have done reality TV, but if you took somebody like Rebekah Vardy, whose only crime seems to have been to marry a footballer, without really ever lauding it up like those WAGS did around the 2006 World Cup, why had she been a target? It is jealousy and nastiness and hate, some of which was probably related to the football.

As far as I could see, she had done nothing wrong. I suspect that when she chose to do *I'm A Celebrity,* she actually did do it so that people could see the real her too. I can't imagine that she needed the money. But that is the measurement of how these people can get under your skin. Individuals whom you don't know and would never meet – until this show – had got at you to such an extent that you felt you had to go and do a reality show to put the record straight. As I had with *Celebrity Big Brother.*

Rebekah Vardy will have also heard it all before at football grounds around the country. Her guy was the star man and that meant she was number one target. But there was something extremely sinister about not being able to see your abuser.

Sam, whom I had heard almost nothing from since seeking my initial advice about going on *X Factor,* had only really started communicating with me again in February 2015. I decided to break the ice and texted her to tell her how sorry I was about her split from Simon Cowell's Syco label.

She had replied that she was 'not upset about it' and added:

'I would have probably been doing another cover album if I'd stayed. I'm glad I've broken free from it all.'

That says a lot. It seems she had tried to tow the line, didn't really agree with what she was being asked to do, and left probably to find her true self. In the process, she too had been attacked online, and it must have been worse for her. She had children for a start.

I thought the show was a cracking idea and hoped it would mark some sort of line in the sand – maybe somebody would pick up on it and speed up the legislation lagging behind the social media revolution. It was still very difficult to get stuff removed and for any further action to be taken.

As preparation, the SAS came to my house! They wanted to see the full extent of how the trolling had affected me. I told them that I had a nervous breakdown and it had destroyed a little piece of me.

I was asked the one question that was key to determine if the show could go ahead:

If they tracked him down, would I confront him?

They left me with two weeks to think about it.

I think the only way to deal with issues like this is to face them. Otherwise it sits there in your sub-conscience and you never deal with it properly, so you cannot be sure when it will come back and haunt you. If you don't make a stand, you will continue to be walked over, and I thought that because a number of individuals were agreeing to take a united front here, the risk of sounding like a born whinger was gone. Intelligent people would see through the venom. In the context of a football match or begging for your vote in a sing-off, yes – it was probably fair game to expect some of the audience to hate you. But in the cold light of day, if this show was well-made, I believed that smart people would make their own minds up. A troll's actions are in the moment. Stripped apart on television and thrown back into their real lives should do the trick.

I was in.

That meant that all roads led to Yeovil in Somerset. I had never done anything like this before. I was heading to a sleepy corner of the country, near where Glastonbury takes place, and where they make cider. I was so far away from home it just added to the randomness of the situation – that somebody so removed from my world, and me theirs, could have taken it upon themselves to target me.

We park up in a car park the night before. I do not know who this guy is. He could be a crazy madman with a knife, a keyboard warrior living with his Mum, or just Mr Ordinary. This is the risk of confrontation – hence why I had back up.

The next day, we head to his house. It is a lovely home in a beautiful area. I really can't quite decide if that makes it worse or better. It is disappointing – I suppose – that what looks on approach as somebody with a nice lifestyle has chosen a style of life that, on the surface, totally contradicts this.

My heart is pumping in a way like never before. I have no idea what I am expecting. My head is racing with a million thoughts. The camera is also rolling. So, I have to consider that I am making a TV show, and how it is coming across. Plus, I have the added element of fearing for my safety, and that I actually do not know what I will say if indeed I do get to go face to face with this troll.

When the producers gave me a fortnight to think about doing the show and you mull it over at home, the one question that you and your partner ask is 'But what will I actually say to them?'

It had occurred to me that less is more – that if I behaved calmly and spoke slowly, then it was all in their reaction…as long as I was safe. I had to back myself and bank on the troll letting themself down.

We arrive at the house. This is it.

I knock on the door. Then, hide in the bush.

We have tried to be discreet in approaching the property. It is not always easy with a camera crew.

There is no answer.

What do we do now? We have a come long way and we have no show or no resolution without the confrontation.

Then, the strangest thing happens. Two vans pull up. A whole load of men get out. They see us, get back in and drive off again. What is all that about?

They don't know we are coming. They have had no time to prepare 'the heavies' to come round and sort us out.

'I'd like to speak to him personally,' I tell the crew.

I knock again.

This time his wife answers – their two little babies behind her. I can see inside their house now. It is a beautiful home. It looks like he runs his own business.

I introduce myself. I say the same to her. I would like to speak to him personally.

'I know who you are, Chris,' she replies, almost sighing that she knew this moment would come.

'I told him not to do it,' she adds. 'And that one day it was going to bite him on the arse.'

She is clearly embarrassed.

I ask her why he had done this. Why did he threaten to kill me? Did he routinely go out and beat up old women? Was this some sort of stress reliever for him as an outlet from his outwardly decent lifestyle? Was this some sort of thrill he was seeking? Did he crave danger?

'It was just something to do,' she apologises, without really seeming to understand it herself.

She calls inside the house to see if he will come to the door.

'He did it more than once,' I reason with her. 'It wasn't just a moment of impulse.'

But she knows. What can she say? It is just mortifying for her and not her fault. He is refusing to come and she is dealing with it on her own doorstep, whilst minding the kids. These people never think it will catch up with them, but now it finally has.

A considerable amount of time had passed since the trolling. He must have thought he was safe from any reprisals, unless he was still doing it to somebody else.

We have reached a stand-off. I could make my case to his wife, but I don't really need to. That is mostly for the cameras. They need to show that I have tried to have dialogue. There is no TV in an unopened door. So, I am not reasoning with her because I expect any answers. We just need footage.

Then, a quite extraordinary moment occurs. His wife passes me the phone. He has agreed to speak to me without meeting.

The ultimate coward would still not come to the door. The keyboard warrior remains hidden.

We speak for fifteen minutes. Initially, he is slow and not forthcoming, leaving me to fill the void. I don't think it matters that the cameras are rolling. His shame is already at a maximum by the fact that I have turned up. Eventually, I goad him into conversation. He finally apologises. I think he realises eventually that the only way to end the conversation is to give me what I want, and that it will be over as soon as I hear the word 'sorry'. I do accept his apology and that is that. There is nothing more to say.

We hang up and I make my way out of his front garden, pumping with adrenaline, but without any concept of how long we have been speaking and having forgotten that it is all on film.

I too had got reeled in. I had done enough TV by now to understand how it works and what they are after, and if I started that conversation on the doorstep knowing that we had to get something, I certainly ended it exorcising my demon and forgetting I was on camera. Just like in the *Big Brother* house, *my* guard was down and that was the real me trying to get answers from my tormentor.

When I got back outside of the property and the crew

congratulated me, it took some time for it to sink in. My head was about to explode as it had done when I arrived, but now with different emotions. I found the whole experience scary but there was no physical threat at all. You see there – the bully almost has the last laugh, that even though I have technically *won,* I only see it as a draw, and I walk away slightly shaken by what I have just done. I can imagine the atmosphere in the troll's house to be quiet – an ashamed silence, with a wife thinking she has three kids, not two on her hands, but he knows too that he has got away with it. There will be no police, no lawsuit of harassment, no repercussions. He endured an uncomfortable half an hour in exchange for all his petty victories over the years. I have a closure, but it leaves me uneasy at best, and recoiling slightly from what I have had to go through to make that happen.

I played back the conversation in my head, asking myself if I got all my points across and revisiting it created anxiety, and I began to wonder if it has been worth it all. I told him that he caused me to have a breakdown. Nobody should put another human being through that. I tried to evaluate his tone when he told me finally that he was sorry. Tone is everything, but then again, how often do people say 'are you sorry or are you just sorry that you got caught?'

We both had a lot of time to think before the show aired. I am sure – gauging his mind from the way he spoke to me – he was dreading the night it was shown. I think it is safe to say that people who knew him would have recognised his wife and front door. How he was ever able to walk through it to the outside world in the days that followed is something I will never know.

Chapter Thirty

By June 2017, I was back in Poland. It had been a while. But an addict is an addict. I decided that I needed my eyes and nose hair doing. On this trip I left Liverpool on the Monday but was home by the Wednesday.

By the time I get back to the house, I had no feeling in my right leg. It was dead. All gone. I don't know what happened. It couldn't have been the flight. It was only two hours to Poland. That was surely not enough time to bring on thrombosis.

Before I knew it, it was not just my leg that had gone. The whole pain was travelling north up to my neck. I was in agony. I told Gary that I thought I was going to die. I had experienced some bad after-effects before, but this propelled itself through my body, and what started with a nagging pain near my foot, shot up like a missile through my entire body. You go to bed thinking it will be fine in the morning, but then wake to find that it is worse.

I was tossing and turning all night, and unable to even hope that it would be gone by the morning. I wasn't about to wake up to some magic nurse in the night, having made it all better because I couldn't bloody sleep. It was killing me – and I literally felt that I was dying. You try to just wait it out, waiting for that sweet relief when you feel the pain finally easing off, but this seemed like there was no way back. It was getting worse, and the only thing I could pinpoint as a possible cause was my addiction to plastic surgery.

For some reason, I just kept going back for more, despite there being disasters, repairs, or just the delayed psychological affects before the pay-off.

By 14 June, my leg was purple, and the rest of my body was covered in yellow bruises. The bills for work had racked up at around £150,000.

I had read many stories about thrombosis and DVT – plenty having arisen from air travel, but I knew that this was

183

not the case. It is one thing when somebody or something injures you, and you know the source and understand why it happened – you can use that knowledge to seek the appropriate treatment – but when you go away to *improve* your body and then come back falling apart and close to death, there really is no comprehension to the lottery of life.

In time, of course, I did recover but, at the time, I saw no end. The bigger picture was that I just could not stop getting my body altered and even though 90 % of it had been an awful experience, by the time I had talked myself into the next round of treatment, enough time had passed that I had allowed the memory of discomfort to pass.

But it wasn't just illness caused by this work. It seemed like misfortune was following me around. Perhaps, if you consider what happened to me on the cruise ships or in the *Celebrity Big Brother* house, I'm not sure whether it is clumsiness or what, but sometimes some people just seem to attract bad luck.

Gary and I were on holiday in Turkey in September 2017. Suddenly I get bitten by a spider. The next thing I know, I am wired up to every machine going and laid low again in a Turkish hospital. For the second time in months, I genuinely thought that I was going to die. Again!

It happened on the beach. I had decided to walk back to the hotel when what felt like a crowbar smacking me on the back of the head knocked me out. My legs, fresh from the recovery after the thrombosis, went as I tried to walk along the front. I was instantly dizzy. I was convinced that I had been attacked – but it was actually only a spider. Groggy, I had fallen to the floor and my throat began to close. I fell straight into shock and only the goodwill and fast thinking of a fellow tourist, named Mandy Fisher, saved me.

I owe Mandy my life. She gave me mouth to mouth and heart compressions and kept me alive until the emergency services arrived. Otherwise, it wouldn't have just been David who was dead. I would have been joining him.

My heart stopped twice. I *was* clinically gone. I

remember almost nothing of what happened. The fact that I had always suffered from arachnophobia is irrelevant. Loads of people are scared of spiders. This just came out of the blue to blind side me, without my knowledge. The spider didn't know I feared them to death. Our paths just happened to cross, and it struck on instinct.

I wondered whether someone from my past had planted the spider. Obviously that's daft, but it did make you wonder how such a random event could befall you. I am also grateful that Gemma Collins wasn't there to give me mouth to mouth.

I am not sure if I would be here to tell the tale without Mandy. As it is, I remain grateful to the ambulance that arrived and picked me up off the street. I just sat there, crying my eyes out, having died on the pavement. My last memory is the ambulance doors shutting on me, and thinking, 'this really is it now.' There seemed like there were about 40 paramedics on the scene. Everybody was there except my Gary.

When the local rep finally tracked him down, he turned up sobbing at the hospital screaming, 'he's dead, isn't he? I know he's dead.' Panic at the incident, the uncertainty of the scale of it, locating the hospital and then finally finding me, plus the uncertainty of not knowing what you would find when you walk through that door are enough to scare the living daylights out of anyone. I, of course, was being seen to in albeit difficult conditions. The worry was more his. Your visiting loved ones are often in the worse state by the time they find you.

And, of course, the last thing you want is to be abroad at a time like this, racking up bills, having everything translated, and with poor Gary just sat there next to me. Clearly there was no holiday after this and we just wanted to get home. I never could track down Mandy Fisher either, who really did save me.

The conditions were not great, either, and I was starting to have that awful feeling that if I didn't get out of here, I might contract something that would make it worse. Let's just say, I craved for the NHS. I'd heard stories in the past of

185

people going to hospital with a minor injury and then getting an infection or something that paralyses them and they end up on their death bed. I looked around the wards where they had taken me, and my concerns just mounted. I told Gary that once they had given me the basic treatment, and I was well enough to walk, then we would get the hell out of there. I had been to the beach, so didn't have all my paperwork on me, which delayed treatment. It seemed like one of those typical 'Brits ill abroad' type shows.

A day later, I discharged myself and spent the rest of the trip in the hotel room, just counting the days to home.

I never wanted to see Turkey or another spider again – though I *might* consider the latter for *I'm a Celebrity!*

Chapter Thirty-One

By now, I had learnt to play the game. What do I mean by that? Well – the spider story ended up in the national press. I knew that if we made it about trying to find Mandy then they would run it, and I was more than happy to go along with it.

The debate therefore resurfaces: do people in the public eye who court the press have the right to shut it down when there is a story they don't like about themselves or when there is a serious case of invasion of privacy?

I understand the argument and I, of course, was nowhere near the level of the Beckhams, for example, who for a time were often accused of the same.

It is a very difficult scenario to speak openly about when you are the subject of the conversation. All I know is that if the press rang me and asked if I was bitten by a spider, what am I supposed to say? There is no point lying, because it happened and they know that, so you might as well go along with it and once you are fully recovered you can then just see it as a bit of fun.

Of course, everybody says there is no such thing as bad publicity – which is total bullshit, by the way – but when you reflect on it, people in the public eye tend to conclude *at the time* that it kept their profile high, and from that, they can do deals, getting invited on chat shows and doing magazine interviews. The way to keep that sweet and to be continued to be invited back on shows like *Lorraine* and *Loose Women,* was to be newsworthy – even though a gay man from Liverpool is bitten by a spider in Turkey is not exactly going to make the end of year review.

So, yes, you go along with it *at the time* and then when something truly awful happens or worse – your privacy is invaded for no genuine reason then this is the stuff that gets thrown back at you later.

The other addition to this argument is that of course, I was fighting back. And where did that start? Well, I had originally been painted as this obscene diva. Then the trolls took over. Subsequently, I had the breakdown. It went quiet for a time, but then the tour began and whispers from inside the camp started once more and several people had jumped on the band wagon. I hadn't fanned or fuelled any of this. Even though I had been 'around' for a few years, we are talking about my first six months or so in 'show business' and I didn't know how it worked. I was playing catch up with a well-oiled machine, and their bed-mates, the tabloids, and then surrounded by a bunch of kids, many of whom were just not mature enough or didn't really care about any consequences.

So, I was way behind the ball-game when I realised even half of what I was up against, and that is why I am so glad I took the decision to go on *Celebrity Big Brother* because that is where perceptions changed.

Remember – I entered the house to boos and came out to cheers, as though nobody remembered the previous show I had been on. That led to other favourable guest slots and, of course, the hugely important trolling programme.

I took that turnaround as a major victory, because if you think back to how that girl from the cruise ship cheaply sold that story about me – a nobody – in the run up to the *X Factor* final of 2012, now I was able to make a call and actually influence some of the nonsense that was going to be written.

Often, I would shake my head that they wanted to print some stuff, and with all the online content, quite often you never even gave an interview. They just reprinted somebody else's. So, if I go on ITV and talk about a tour or plastic surgery or my academy, then one of the journalists run it, and half the time it doesn't even make the press but, it stays on Google forever.

There is of course, one benefit to that. It helps me write this book!

But it wasn't just spiders. The press would run anything that would sell papers. I recognise that the goalposts had also moved for them too. Historically, it had been about those big Sunday exclusives in papers like the now defunct *News of the World,* but now it was about hits on your website and clickbait. There was not a set number of pages in one edition anymore. Just fill your website. It was more a case of churning everything and, if Christopher Maloney had a car crash, then people might click on it.

As it happened I had two:

I was driving to Blackpool for *Peter Pan* with Kurtis Stacey from *Emmerdale,* when I fell foul of a drunk driver, trying to get into a non-existent third lane, crashing into me who then went into somebody else, whilst the drunk driver hit the kerb, nearly taking out some pedestrians. Our dog went through the windscreen.

The airbags failed and I was knocked unconscious. Gary was already out on the street, helping others, before he could see the full extent of me slumped across the wheel.

Kurtis took himself off to the press day. I was left to help police with their enquiries.

He jumped out, whilst we were receiving First Aid. Gary and I were in a bad way. There was no way I could attend. These things take hours to clear up, and then we had to go to the police station, where they handed me my personal affects, rescued from the wreck. We were left with no way home. Apart from the physical discomfort, it was crushing to know that you had done nothing wrong, but now had to summon a taxi back to Blackpool, looking like an actual car wreck, and waiting for Gary's brother to come and fetch us.

There was a theme developing here. Blackpool seemed to be the common denominator, but it really did seem that when I was about to open an exciting new chapter, somebody would throw a spanner in the works.

In July 2017, I was following a transit van when its ladders came loose, hitting the highway and smashing into my car. One minute I am driving along, humming to the radio, thinking about the day ahead and how exciting it was that I was finally on my way to record my second single, and the next thing I think I am going to die again. Anybody who has had a crash thinks that for a split second, but actually I was relatively OK. The people following me, who smashed in to the back of me, were worse off.

I spun into the hard shoulder and had one of those 'life flashes before you' moments. A couple of months previously, I had dreamt that this would happen. As you know, that is not the first time that has happened. I was left with four broken ribs.

Hardly ideal when you are about to go and sing your lungs out.

By February 2018, I was on a 42-date tour of *Dance To The Music,* with Kristina Rihanoff. I was staying at the *Holiday Inn* and went to the toilet in the night. I told the press that I had gone to the toilet, but given I was on my own, there was no need to lock the door. Actually, I went for a sly cigarette. The handle fell off and suddenly I was locked in, which was not great, considering I have a history of claustrophobia issues. Nobody heard my cries, of course. The heater was on full blast. There were no windows. There was a real danger my new face could melt! Seriously though, I panicked.

I was banging and screaming for over an hour – my hands red raw and badly bruised from trying to raise the alarm. To no avail. I had little choice but to give up and make a bed of towels for the night. By morning somebody had come to the room.

It was starting to get a bit ridiculous. In February 2018, I was now homeless and living in my car. Except, I wasn't, of course.

The press stated that I had *lost* my home and was living in my Mercedes. Why would you therefore not sell the car?!

There it was – that tabloid picture of me removing bin bags from the vehicle! And a sleeping bag.

The truth was somewhat different, so I responded by saying that actually I was living in hotels, but my car had broken down.

But this time, I was not party to the story. Somebody at

the theatre knew my car was knackered and must have alerted a paparazzo. They knew exactly when my car was leaving, and it was there to see – me looking humiliated, being towed back to Liverpool.

Homeless however, I was not.

Of course, these stories are all mumbo-jumbo really – and as I mentioned before, 'today's news, tomorrow's chips', except that no longer applied with Google. More so – today's fake news embedded in tomorrow's microchips.

They mean little, irritate you sometimes when the facts are totally off the planet, and nobody is interested in correcting them. When there is a sense of betrayal about them, then you really are on your guard and feel pretty disgusted.

The key though is that none of them are really personal. They haven't actually invaded the space of people in my life. But I just knew that they would at some point.

Back in January 2015, Gary and I had gone to Egypt to get engaged. We had flown Danniella out for a bit of fun. Rosie Gizauskas in *Heatworld* wrote, 'Congrats, Maloney – at least you won't have to hire a wedding singer. You can do the warbling yourself'. It just seemed like a nasty, stupid thing to write – but look at the date.

I have saved this one to last deliberately. It pre-dates the change in attitude to me. It is a comment made after *X Factor,* but before *Celebrity Big Brother.* One journalist, whom I had never met just assumed the tone adopted by all the others, based on the drip feed of mis-information and rumour from the show. She doesn't even call me by my Christian name, and the word 'warbling' is clearly used to be deliberately cutting.

Then she goes on to suggest that Danniella has just weirdly turned up, as though she was outstaying her welcome. We invited her! Then there is a dig where she implies that after seeing pictures on my Twitter, it looks like I have actually got engaged to Dani…but oh no, we forgot for a moment that Christopher is gay.

It pitches Danniella as a gatecrasher and us as

tacky...'Danniella sits astride a camel with a neon pink bikini on, and it's just kind of weird'.

There is no quality to this article. She just thinks she is safe, because everyone else was printing similar rubbish. I have not received this kind of nastiness since *Big Brother,* however.

Google may mean these stories do stay forever now, but they also can expose some pretty shite journalism too. And that in some cases, is the only accountability because, just like the troll programme, the public can see for themselves.

Of course, by the end of the next year, we hear, Gary and I had split. David is dead. No he isn't. Gary and I had split. No, we hadn't.

A source told *The Sun* that we were, 'both devastated that it hasn't worked out after eight years together'.

I am sorry, but I do not discuss this kind of thing with anybody and everybody, so there could not possibly be any source. It is an old cliché in the press that 'a journalist will never reveal their sources'. It is pitched as a line of integrity to ensure the confidant's identity will not be compromised in light of the sensitivity of a story, and also to show that the writer can be trusted and has really good contacts, only available to them.

What it does not say to you is the other truth. A source means that they can just make it up if they want to:

'They were solid at the beginning of the year when Christopher was in the *Celebrity Big Brother* house but since then things haven't been good. More details are bound to emerge but now the wedding is very much off'.

Realistically, that source could only have been Gary or myself. It was neither.

Interestingly, as I write these words today, Gary is sat next to me, and neither of us can find any story anywhere that we have un-split, have been re-joined at the hip, are back in love etc etc...

Christopher and Gary have split. Christopher and Gary have not split. I will leave you to make your own mind up.

Chapter Thirty-Two

I do not know what the future holds. There are no guarantees in life, obviously. I would expect there will lots more Gary, a fair bit more panto, and one or two more new faces! Plus, the usual diet of tabloid nonsense, until I fall out with them or have exhausted my small amount of fame. Hopefully the good fun will continue on some of my favourite ITV shows, like *Lorraine* and *Loose Women*. I doubt that I will be asked back on the spin-off *Big Brothers* shows – not because we have fallen out or I have smacked Gemma Collins's arse with a wet kipper live on TV, but mainly because at the time of writing, it looks like it has come to the end of its life.

It was an iconic programme – a real game changer when fellow Scouser, Craig Phillips, won it in its opening year in a series that became known for Nasty Nick's dirty tricks. In various guises on a couple of channels, it has had nearly two decades and propelled many people into showbiz, and just about kept a few others hanging on!

I am sad if it has gone for the final time, but I am absolutely delighted that I had the opportunity, and will always reflect that our year was a particularly extraordinary series. We owe that to the two Davids.

For me personally, it is a measurement in that awful word of my 'journey' that everyone uses on all these shows and, as I try to complete it here, by bringing it as up to date as I can before publication, there is almost only one place to conclude it.

Back on *Loose Women* in the summer of 2018. I am there to discuss one thing – the surgery. A show that I have been working on for *Channel 5* called *Celebrities In Therapy* is due to air in the September. I had also the previous month undergone further work with more Botox, teeth re-construction and another nose job. I think, only Michael Jackson had more.

I explained to them again that it had been the trolling

that had driven me to it, to which Janet Street-Porter replied that she didn't conform to a standard celebrity look, but had found a way past the keyboard warrior.

I told them that I liked how I looked now, but couldn't look at myself in a mirror for any length of time. That was always my reaction in the weeks that followed and then just as I started to accept it and like it, I would go again. Nobody had ever told me to stop but, like anything, it can become an addiction and I had to face facts that I now had a serious dependency.

I told them that it did make me feel good – but therein lies the problem. I had resorted to a physical response in answer to a mental problem. Christine Bleakley suggested that instead of surgery, I needed therapy. That, of course, was the project I had been working on.

They made me look in the mirror on national TV. I had never done anything like this before. I lasted three seconds before turning away.

'Chris, you're shaking,' Janet consoled me.

Christine piped in, making me promise that I would get therapy before undergoing any more surgery:

'You don't need any more,' she added. 'You're perfect as you are. We will be checking up on you.'

These were words which were beyond kind. I was not and am not perfect, and I felt a million miles away from it – hence the need for desperate measures. They could have slaughtered me on this show. The whole Diva thing could have re-surfaced. They were right about one thing.

I did need to talk. So, for the second time, I had taken my personal issue in front of the cameras and signed up to the *Channel 5* show.

For four months, they came to my house every two weeks and filmed me, then made a one-hour show. Obviously, they had to cut loads out. But they left the key bits in. I think it is a very American experience to air your soul in public, but we are getting more and more used to it in this country. It is very easy to say that you hope the show helps somebody else. I do feel that, because a few of us did the troll show hoping that that might be the case. But, essentially when you sit down to talk to the therapist on a show like this, you once again forget the cameras are rolling, so you hope that you are making a TV show, and obviously you are getting a fee, and if it helps somebody else, then great. Regardless of all that, I think this was the first time I had sat down properly, with somebody qualified, to talk to over a period of time – a lady by the name of Mandy Saligari – and that was the most important point.

I told her much of what I have written here. Expressing it both in print and talking one to one has given me clarity, if not closure.

I have pinpointed much of what happened to me at the door of the troll, which was left wide open by my experiences on the *X Factor*. The reality, of course, is that we are a product of the collective, and whatever it is in that show that exposed me as vulnerable, is a by-product of everything since day one in life.

So, I talked to Mandy about dreams – how all I wanted to do as a kid was do impressions, sing, dance and act, but Dad wanted me to go to boxing, rather than drama school, and that bullying started at school where I was a 'queer' with a girly voice. Ironically, they knew I was gay before I did.

Even though Mandy seemed to have the answers to most things, some of the circumstances in which she finds them still baffle her. Here was her first conclusion: that I had anger at the non-intervention from the adult world, which has placed me as a victim, that the system had failed me and that I was crying out for intervention that never came.

I do not remember feeling like that at the time. I just felt like I was a victim and that I *was* different for being gay. It takes the passage of time to fully understand how you wish it had been dealt with.

Mandy asked me if I had seen *X Factor* as a launch pad to something else. I told her that all I wanted to do was stand on that X and that my ambition was complete. In isolation, it sounds a stupid concept. I think she understood that was the summit of my ambition, but could see that, in the bigger picture, it meant little. When I said that the dream was complete, she just nodded as if to say that I had a long way to go to really understand both myself and what were realistic goals in life.

Then we reached a trigger point. The judges' comments had been pivotal in all this, before the trolling started. That was a narrative in cyberspace that followed on from what people saw in the show. Week in week out, those remarks hurt. Watching a compilation years later confirmed, at least to me, that, for the most part, there appeared to be no substance or credibility to them, but it was the tone and avoidance in them that killed me. The former was that underlying mocking, and the latter was that there were no comments about my vocals, other than when prompted as an after thought. It was all about stuff that was out of my control, like staging and song choice.

The word control is, of course, a key word, in therapy. I told her that I felt now that that the comments were 'playground' – the theme prevails from the childhood bullying. She was amazed at what she called my compliance.

Then we looked at the threats that followed – 'I'm gonna slit your throat' and 'stab your Nan in the back'. She confirmed that it was the anonymity of the keyboard warrior that was key to the venom.

I told her that this was the moment when I decided that I could not look myself in the mirror any more. Those big eyes of wonder which people saw on the first audition had lost their sparkle and, even though I didn't turn to it immediately, it was the beginning of the route to plastic surgery.

She spoke words I had never considered before:

'The world turned on you. It's like you turned on you too. You joined them. You agreed.'

It was true. I had an enormous amount of self-loathing. I explained that I actually did not want the surgery, and that my friends had advised me against it and told me that I didn't need it, but that I *felt* that I did not have a choice, which is really stupid. People say that perception is reality, but how had

196

I got myself into a situation where I had convinced myself that I was the only person who was right and that people I knew and loved were not to be listened to?

'I can only imagine what it must be like, feeling like all these people…who at one moment are giving you a standing ovation, and then having the feeling that you have been ripped apart, and when you look in the mirror…all you are going to do is agree with them.'

I liked the way she put that.

As I am explaining all this to Mandy, she tells me to take a breath. She can see the anxiety in me and says it is almost transferring to her and is painful to watch.

'I felt like I needed to do it. It became an obsession,' I confessed.

Her response was smart – that many men also now undergo a lot of surgery in what was once mainly the woman's territory. For whatever reason, people had lost sight of who they were, and were concentrating on what they looked like, and that I did it for that reason, because, in my mind, I felt robbed emotionally – that I had followed a dream, done nothing wrong, but the system had decided that the world would turn against me. She said it was understandable that I felt resentful, even though I hadn't used the word, but she explained that resentful was a sentiment akin to an emotional cancer.

'You joined them,' she clarified. 'You agreed with them.'

It was one way of looking at it. She put it calmly and succinctly, but it shows how complicated the brain is, because there was no way that I *did* agree with them, but my compliance, my submission, indicated so.

The next bit is hard to hear. She concluded that because I had been sincere, but had felt like I had had the piss taken out of me, I then had entered into a victim state…a 'poor me' state.

I only actually entered a talent competition. Sometimes people say *you* play the victim. You might have read about the

197

spider or the car crash and thought my life *was* a car crash, and that I wanted some sort of sympathy, but these are events that happened to me. I did not magic them from nowhere. This was the first time that I had heard the words 'you have entered a victim state' and it crushed me a little, because it does sound like either a chosen path, in that it is what you wanted all along, or one in which you were so weak, you pathetically subsided.

I hope the truth is neither, and that bullying as a child has nothing to do with my desire to perform in the arts, and when I thought I had the dream in my hands, the bullying returned and I spiralled. To me, the two were separate, but then became intertwined without me knowing so.

She explained that I had been reduced to a mindset where I felt like it didn't matter what I did, because they were are all going to hate me anyway – and I do recognise that does seem like a victim scenario, and I had created a defensive position in response to questions.

We analysed the diva comments – in particular the fact that today, there was now the spiralling effect of a comment made once on a TV show, then had legs through other media and was repeated so often that it became a truth. That did conform to the old advertising adage that it was not what you said but how many times you said it, and that if you tell somebody something enough times they will accept it as a truth. But that concept now played in the multi-platform modern world.

'What do you think of fame at any price?' Mandy asked me.

'I just wanted to sing,' I re-iterated. 'I didn't want fame.'

I realise that it comes with the territory, but if you strip it back to the first time you heard a song on the radio that you loved, and you sung along and thought that is something you would love to do, you are not attracted to celebrity. It is melody and harmony and words and delivery – and even though some people do want to be famous for being famous, I

198

just wanted to express myself in a performance arena.

As she asked me again about fame, my heart began to race with a pressure that took me back to the *X Factor* – a feeling I never felt on the stage, but always felt around it. Mandy observed that I was breathless, defensive, self-pitying and retreating into a corner – a position whose origin is at childhood.

When I watched the show back it was exhausting. It was very difficult to know if I had been short-changed, because we had done so many hours of talking on camera, but I accept that is the edit. I think it is very raw, but credible. Even though there were contributions from my sister, Mum and Gary, along with clips from the past, I think it would have been a better show without them. I say this – defensively – because they had one counter opinion on there, in the form of a journalist, James Ingham, Showbiz Editor at the *Daily Star on Sunday,* who admitted that he didn't know if all the stories that came out of *X Factor* were true, but that he believed my 'behaviour was appalling at times'.

To me, I think those comments reeked of contradiction and fall short of credible. Some of the stuff you hear and read may not true, but oh yes, Chris was a shocker.

I leave you to decide.

The show ends with a conclusion, but it is very hard to then take those thoughts and revelations back into the real world. But, Mandy did help me understand my defensiveness, and my role in my own misery, and even though I protested that I did not see myself as a victim, she explained that the word could be defined into two categories.

Either I was thinking 'why are you doing that to me' or 'I am so shit, I can see why you are doing that to me?' I am not allowed to step out of the hard done by mentality because then everyone will have a go at me again. Her conclusion was that I had to learn to tell myself that I was good enough, I am allowed these emotions, and that I didn't have to justify myself – which, of course, I have just done.

Chapter Thirty-Three

That was then. This is now. They were the words that I signed off with to Mandy at the end of the show. I probably should watch an edited version back once a week. It would probably serve me well. I thought she was compassionate, friendly but most of all fair – appalled by some of the nonsense that had come my way, analytical of how it had set me back, together with the disappointment, rejection, helplessness I felt.

If I had just sounded off to her and they had re-hashed old footage, then even though Mandy was very, very good, it would have lacked the balance required. So, I had to take some harsh lessons from it, which was difficult at first, but I'm now happy that I did. The problem, which I am sure Mandy will confirm, is that people often conform to type and make the same mistakes over again, and are drawn to the same set of circumstances.

I think there was one key piece of evidence that suggested that I could break the cycle – confronting the troll would help me go a long way forward, and what that future would mean, I wouldn't know.

As I conclude this book, I read today that I have gone missing (October 2018) after getting 'robbed and failing to turn up at a gig. My best friend, Mark Byron, tweeted that he was worried sick about me after our boozy Champagne lunch in Soho. Another friend, Gemma Oaten, later confirmed that she had heard from me and I was very much alive. In July, I had also been mugged, whilst stopping for fuel in Stafford, leaving me badly bruised and with a black eye. The pictures looked almost as bad as after some of my surgeries.

I appear to be typing this, after all, and with a massive smile on my face. Is that kind of nonsense news a measurement of how far we have come since 2012? Not really, in that you can't get hold of people sometimes in life, but the fact that papers and social media deemed it newsworthy is a hell of a long way from the first time that I walked onto that X just wanting to sing.

That is where it all started and will never end. I am a singer, first and last, and 2019 means that I will be back on the road again, out on tour and in the recording studio. And who knows after that.

I have learned a lot, was given an incredible opportunity, and like to think I took it with both hands and made the most of everything that followed, despite the angst, heartache, injury and chaos along the way. But I am still going and 2019 means a UK theatre tour, more TV shows planned and, of course, panto!

Not bad for a *Wildcard.*

I will leave the last word to Dan Wootton, now Executive Editor at *The Sun,* who wrote in the summer of 2018 that I was the latest Z-lister to release an autobiography, something which entertained me greatly, given how much he has penned about me over the years. Obviously, I was mortified to be called a Z lister. I hoped by now that I had made it up to Y, but obviously Dan knows best and works his craft so hard to get all those *X Factor* stories over the years, so who am I to argue?

Describing this as a 'new addition to the books-the-world-never-needed shelf' and being released, 'despite no obvious public demand', he quotes me as saying, 'It's warts and all.'

That is terrific, because he truly got something right! I did put that in the press release. I have actually not been misquoted. We were finally getting somewhere.

And I guess that if one person buys this other than my Mum, sister, Nan, and my Gary then there has been a public demand beyond Dan's wildest dreams.

Obviously, on a personal level, it has helped as, with Mandy's work, to put it all down and to reflect on some of the madness of it all, but only you can decide if Dan got it right or not. Unless you have done that thing where you flick to the back page in a bookstore, I am assuming that you have read all the way through. Maybe, just once, Dan was wrong!

Obviously, I should not have promised that it was warts and all. I had better give that plastic surgeon another call!!!

CPSIA information can be obtained
at www.ICGtesting.com
Printed in the USA
BVHW030907231118
533823BV00001B/56/P